BAD MOMMY

Also by Willow Yamauchi:

Adult Child of Hippies

BAD MOMMY

Willow Yamauchi

INSOMNIAC PRESS

Library and Archives Canada Cataloguing in Publication

Yamauchi, Willow
Bad mommy / Willow Yamauchi.

ISBN 978-1-55483-066-4
Ebook ISBN 978-1-55483-079-4

1. Motherhood--Humor. I. Title.

PN6231.M68Y34 2012   306.874'30207   C2012-900764-1

The publisher gratefully acknowledges the support of the Canada
Council, the Ontario Arts Council and the Department of
Canadian Heritage through the
Book Publishing Industry Development Program.

Printed and bound in Canada

Insomniac Press
520 Princess Avenue, London, Ontario, Canada, N6B 2B8
www.insomniacpress.com

Canada Council   Conseil des Arts
for the Arts   du Canada

ONTARIO ARTS COUNCIL
CONSEIL DES ARTS DE L'ONTARI

Canada

This book is a work of humour and is not intended as parenting advice. This book is not meant to be used, nor should it be used, to diagnose or treat any medical condition.

Although these are the stories of real mommies, names and identifying information have been changed to protect the innocent, as well as the guilty.

Acknowledgement

A special thank you to all the brave mommies who chose to tell their stories here. Thanks also to my patient and loving husband, Ron, and my forgiving and hilarious kids, Sophie and Flynn. Thank you to my publisher, Mike O'Connor, for giving me a chance to tell my crazy stories, and a big thanks to my editor, Gillian Urbankiewicz, for helping me get it right.

Dedication

This book is dedicated to Grandma Gladys, who hated kids but loved me anyway; Grandma Fay, who told me that mommies lie because they have to; and my own mommy, Sharon, who taught me everything I know.

Table of Contents

Introduction

Women are expected to embrace the beautiful gift of becoming a mommy. Giving birth, nourishing our young: these things are the fulfillment of a life's ambition. You'll be spoken of in the same breath as patriotism and apple pie. There you'll be on a pedestal—admired, happy. All you have to do is be a good mommy.

The cruel truth is being a good mommy is pretty much impossible. This creature exists only as a figment of our collective hope that we can actually be everything that our families need us to be. We all try to be good.

And the truth is you will fail. Oh, not at all of it, hopefully, or even most, probably. This is not about evil mommy; this book is by, about, and for the many women who are somewhere between Joan Crawford and June Cleaver. Chances are you already know things you didn't do right, but what are the other things you are always wondering about?

Wonder no longer. This book will map out the various pitfalls awaiting the soon-to-be bad mommy. This is not to help you avoid them…not really. What kind of an insane promise is that? No, this is not about avoidance, but commiseration. While there is no way to avoid the impossible tasks and unfair tests along your path, you may derive the modest consolation that comes from knowing that you are not alone.

In fact, in this book, no fewer than twenty-two admitted bad mommies will share their fears and disappointments with you.

With your first pregnancy, you will likely read every book you can on parenting: *On Becoming Baby Wise*, *What to Expect When You're Expecting*. Each promises to be your Bible. These books are full of lies and must be read with extreme incredulity. Where you once thought of friends, career, and sex, you will now be devoting brain cells to the memorization of charts, milestones, and trends. All of these resources are part of a secret practical joke designed to expose you for the maternal sham that you really are. You will try your best, but you will fail.

Let's face it, unless you are seriously deluded, deep down you already know that you are a bad mommy, don't you? Let's speak frankly, shall we? Some of us hide it better, but every woman—especially those who seem to have it all under control—will have to admit that in her deepest heart badness is her evil truth.

Instead of hiding mommy guilt and shame with

brave smiles, matching mother-daughter outfits, and three o'clock martinis, in *Bad Mommy* we celebrate our neuroses, shortcomings, and nasty little habits. Only *Bad Mommy* dares to tell the truth. Make yourself a cup of tea, pour a hot bath, and brace yourself for the secrets of your true future and what to fear when you are expecting.

Chapter 1

Baby Bad Mommy and Crone Bad Mommy

It's never the right time to buy real estate. The more a person thinks it over and dissects her choice, the less likely she will be to actually take the plunge.

It's the same with pregnancy. Ignorance, truly, is bliss. The act of getting pregnant puts you on an adventure that is both dramatic and permanent: once the train has left this particular station, there will be no turning back.

Nor is admission based on rationality since pregnancy can happen early: old enough to bleed, old enough to breed.

Give or take the odd cult, modern humans no longer encourage their young to have babies and laws exist to protect our young from predatory adults. Although our bodies may be ready when we are thirteen, we generally realize that our tempers and responsibilities are not ready until substantially later…which raises other problems.

If Mommy has her child too early, there is no way that she will have been able to establish her career and education prior to childbirth. She will be trapped in the mommy gulag of minimum wage or welfare, and her children will be cursed with her financial ineptitude and most likely lack of Baby Daddy. People will perpetually think Young Bad Mommy is the older sister of her own children, and delivery people will ask to speak to the "lady of the house," looking around her shoulder hopefully as she opens the door.

Too Young Bad Mommy's body probably did not finish filling out by the time she gave birth. The fetus will rob her growing body of precious nutrients, damning Too Young Bad Mommy to a life of early osteoporosis and cronedom.

Too young bad mommies are also not accepted by the regular mommies who are disdainful of her jumping the queue to mommyhood. She may have the children to prove that she is a mommy, but if she doesn't have the years behind her, she will never rate and her status with other mommies will be pariah-like. Sure they will be friendly to her at play group but she will never earn an invitation over to their home for coffee later. Never.

Should Mommy delay her breeding a few years into her mid twenties, an age thought by many to be ideal for childbirth, she will be more likely to be accepted by the other mommies, as she has moved beyond the distasteful "girl bride" phase of her life. However, having children at this age is a career killer. Most people complete their education and establish careers in their twenties. A woman who chooses this phase of her life to have children will be firmly stepping into the "mommy track" at work. Her potential for career advancement will be nil, as she will be red-circled as a problematic breeder who will likely be taking incessant maternity leaves and time off to deal with her snot-nosed progeny. Yes, mid-aged Mommy will have the energy for her children (hypothetically) and she will not die of old age before they finish high school, but mid-aged Bad Mommy will do this at her own expense. She passes the success baton on to her own children early, as she will not be able to fulfill her own dreams if she embraces mommyhood at this stage in her life.

Bad Mommies who wait until their thirties to have children are playing with fire. Yes, they will have now established a career and likely finished their education. They may even have a few dollars in the bank. However, this is one of the most dangerous times of all to have children. Once you are set in your path as a career woman, it is very hard to change gears. Your employer has built up a trust in you and is dependent on the knowledge that you are not one of those flighty young girls ready to go out there and propagate—and now this!

The pressure on Thirties Mommy to have a baby is huge. People start to get anxious as the big breeding clock winds down. Better get those eggs plugged before they rot! Thirties Mommy also gets to experience the joy of multiple invasive pregnancy tests. The experts agree: the wrinklier the mommy, the more likely it is that her baby will end up as a late-term abortion.

The new mommy in her forties is perhaps the baddest of all. For a woman to have her first child in her forties, something has gone seriously amiss with her breeding schedule. Maybe she was waiting for Mr. Right, or dallied the years away with Mr. Right Now. Most likely, though, her late blooming desire to get pregnant is due to her slavish obsession with career advancement and/or hedonistic pursuits and now she's clamping down onto any spare semen in desperation. Or she made a conscious choice to not have children for almost two decades and then changed her mind in a last-minute hysterical effort to leave her genetic mark on this earth.

While older mommies do have the resources to financially support a young child, their own physical resources are dwindling. Even if the child is born free of Down Syndrome or some other genetic malady, their mommy will have little energy to play with them. Instead of chasing the wee tot around the playground, Crone Mommy will soon be lying on the bench, spent, with images of her halcyon thirties floating amongst the starry specks.

Crone Mommy will lead an isolated life, with the vast majority of her peers having either had their children or made the decision to go childfree. By the time her baby is wearing Pull-Ups, the children of her friends will be getting ready for their proms. Mommies her age will not be eager to revisit the unsanitary chaos of the pre-toilet years, while younger mommies with similar-aged children may feel daunted by Crone Mommy's higher socioeconomic status and creeped out by her age spots. Crone Mommy's children's memories will be underpopulated, and also short, as she will orphan them in their early twenties.

Kitty is a twenty-seven-year-old mother of a six-year-old boy and two-year-old girl, and she is twenty-eight weeks pregnant. Kitty had her first child when she was twenty years old. She can recall a customer coming up to her and saying, "Oh my God, you're pregnant! You are way too young to have a baby." She kept repeating it over and over. Finally a co-worker said "we all thought she was a little young when she got married" as though the marriage excused the tender years. Kitty will never forget the shame she felt: "I was totally embarrassed, absolutely humiliated, shocked." After that comment, Kitty felt that everyone was watching her and judging her age. Her in-laws suggested that at least she was getting this pregnancy "over with" so that she could go back to work.

Six years later, Kitty still feels a schism with older mommies. Just last week at her son's school, one of the crone mommies made a disparaging remark about a new teacher: "She's really, really, really young. She's got to be as young as you!" Kitty likes to dress in trendy clothes and doesn't drive a minivan. Her child goes to school with a mohawk or green hair, and that's just fine with her. The older mommies don't want to be friends with Kitty, but that's OK because Kitty doesn't want to be friends with them either.

Lilah, age thirty-seven, had her two-year-old son twelve days after she turned thirty-five. "Age thirty-five puts you in a higher risk group, especially if it's your first." Lilah got to experience first-hand the joys of multiple invasive tests during pregnancy with ambiguous and potentially threatening results. After learning that her son was in fact shockingly NOT stricken by some terrible malady because of her aging eggs, she still had a lot to learn about being an old bad mommy. Lilah and her partner felt out of place in their Lamaze classes, which were full of young couples barely in their twenties. As a teacher, Lilah realized that the other parents in the class seemed "like children"—often arriving late, and never with completed birthing homework.

After her son was born, Lilah pushed on to join a Mother Goose group. These groups are designed to teach inept bad mommies how to sing to their children. Again there were no friends her age in sight. Lilah realized that most of the other mommies in the group were wearing T-shirts that in some way referenced beer. The other mommies didn't want to be her friend, and she didn't want to hang out with them and their beer shirts either. It was a bit of a mommy stand off. Lilah is hopeful that she will meet some decent mommies now that her child is attending daycare.

Chapter 2

Bad Mommy Times Her Pregnancies

Whatever path you have taken as a mommy, you have erred. Accept this now. Should you be one of those few, somewhat annoyingly perfect mommies who actually thoughtfully planned their pregnancies and did not run into mutant eggs or feeble sperm, you can feel confident that you will make a mistake somewhere in the course of parenting. Like buying property or getting married, there is no consensus on the right time to have children. You will be too young or too old, too poor, too busy, or too selfish. One might as well ask for the right time to jump off a cliff.

Once you have done the deed and created a new human life to burden the ecosystem and infect with your neuroses, the first question on many minds will be when you'll do it again. Should you doom your first-born to being an only child? The only child is an impoverished freak with no siblings to play with and develop social skills. These children become parentified miniature adults and have no interest in playing with other children, which causes social developmental delays. This will all translate into immature relationship styles as adults, leading to countless hours on the therapist's couch all because of Bad Mommy's selfish and short-sighted decision not to bless her child with a younger sibling.

Of course, should you decide to spare your darling the horror of being an only child, you are now condemning your perfect first-born to a life of drudgery, harnessed forever with an albatross of a younger sibling who will undoubtedly ruin your first-born child's once-perfect life forever. Every parent of a second child wonders—correctly—if they have made a huge mistake by tempting fate. Sure, you have the "heir and a spare," but now both children have half the resources of a single child. They can go to university half as long and have half as large a down payment on their first home. This, of course, compounds with even more children: each subsequent egg fertilization is an economic knife in your first child's back.

When timing their children, bad mommies have many opportunities to develop deep-set neuroses and guilt complexes. If you space out your children more than three years, they will not develop as true peers and will have a shallow and antagonistic relationship. If you have them less than three years apart, neither child will have your undivided attention, nor will they have the mental and financial resources they need. Better yet, have twins! Here is a surefire way to make sure that both children are losing out equally.

If at all possible, one should strive to have a child's birthday land on a very important holiday or, better yet, another family member's birthday, allowing for bad feelings all around.

Birthdays are the gift that keeps on giving. Have a child in summer and your child will have no friends around for the party. Have your child before Christmas and not enough time will have passed for true friendships to develop in class, causing a sad and shallow birthday party. Extra bonus guilt of having a child who is too young for their class and will always be delayed behind their January and February birthday cohorts. Have a child from January to May and your child will be too old for their classroom and will be thwarted with feelings of inadequacy as classmates a full year younger are doing the same classwork. They get to be the first to develop during puberty, the first to try adult vices, and the first to explore other opportunities for leadership.

A personal favourite is the notion that mommies should "try" for a specific gender with their second-born child. As you nuzzle your newborn daughter, your thoughtful mother-in-law might suggest that you try for a boy next time. The message in these statements is clear: you have failed by producing a child of the wrong gender. Some families try and try and try again to get that elusive other gender and never succeed. The message to your wrong-gendered child is clear, and the ensuing gender confusion, guilt, and paranoia will be nicely transferred onto future generations with your flagrant "trying."

When Sally, a forty-year-old mother of an eight-year-old boy, found out that she was expecting her second child, she was "stunned, stunned, stunned." For years, she and her husband had been trying for another child, but had since resigned themselves that this was not going to happen. "The very week before I found out I was pregnant, I found out how to refer my husband for a vasectomy—great timing!" As eight years had passed since the birth of her last child, she had given away all of her baby things and maternity clothes.

Sally's husband, aged fifty-seven, has two grown children from previous marriages. He has been planning for his retirement in three years. "Oh my God, I will be poor, with an old retired husband," she told me. "I had this one perfect child and now he's going to have less."

With older siblings aged eight, twenty-three, and twenty-five, Sally's new baby will have siblings born in three different decades. Sally's twenty-three-year-old stepdaughter was less than impressed upon hearing of her newest baby sibling. "This one better be a fucking girl...when are you guys going to be responsible?" Sally is too embarrassed to tell the twenty-five-year-old, who is very interested in being a "mature and responsible adult," about the impending arrival.

Bridget, a forty-two-year-old mother of a seven-year-old girl and four-year-old boy, reports "weird pressure not to have an only child" as soon as she had her first. There were incessant questions about her plans to get pregnant again. "Like I'm ever going to have sex again to make a baby!" she laughs. The irony!

Bridget's children are three years apart, not the commonly accepted appropriate spacing of one to two years. Anything more than one to two years and you are on your own. If there are any problems, it's your fault. If children are too far apart in age, they will never play together properly. The older sibling will be thrust into role of the "parent" and true intimacy will not develop between siblings.

Once Bridget bit the bullet and had a second child, she was somewhat scandalized by comments from the peanut gallery: "You are so lucky, you had one of each... congratulations!" and "You had a BOY this time!" Although everyone seems to agree that two children of the same gender is optimal, everyone also seems to agree that one of each is also optimal, so at least there is a good chance of success regarding gender selection.

Chapter 3

Bad Single Mommy

Remember mommies: being a mommy is all about meeting other people's needs, not your own. However, if you are in a relationship with someone whose needs you can never meet, you many need to get out. Fifty percent of all marriages are not successful; that means an awful lot of mommies are currently living in misery with their partners, and an awful lot of mommies will be single at some point in their mommy careers.

By staying in an unhealthy relationship, Mommy is showing her children how to behave when they are in adult relationships. If she models negative and anti-social interactions, her children will pick up on these cues and will use them in their own relationships as adults, thus dooming future generations to unhealthy and unloving family life cycles. Bad Mommy who stays in a bad relationship will teach her children that her own happiness, and by extension their own happiness, is not as important as the institution of marriage.

If, however, Mommy should decide to leave her

relationship, she will permanently scar her children for life. Her young will become Ping-Pong balls flitting across the town on some hare-brained visitation schedule that no one can ever seem to keep straight. They will never be invited to overnight birthday parties because they will inevitably land on the night they are supposed to be in their other home. Children of divorce—except in extremely rare cases—are deeply insecure, as their attachment figures are not constant.

By not doing the tough work to work it out and stay in an abusive and loveless relationship, Bad Divorced Mommy will have committed herself and her child to a lifetime of overnight bags and vacation-date anxieties. As well, should she and/or her ex hook up with someone else, there will be the charming issue of step-mommies to contend with. There is nothing like a new mommy for your child to make you realize what a bad mommy you really are! Maybe the new mommy will be younger, more hip, more interested in child-related activity. Maybe your child will want to go and live with your ex and his new harlot—full-time! What about if subsequent half-siblings are born to either you or your ex-spouse? Bad Mommy's child position in the household will forever be threatened by new baby siblings who, by their very presence, have usurped the original child of the relationship that is no more.

Some bad mommies decide to become single

parents by choice. Single wannabes can either adopt or find themselves a donor and go it alone. This is clearly an insane choice. Without another parent, whom can Mommy blame? Parenting is difficult enough with two functional parents. Planning to go it alone to meet your own needs for procreation at the expense of a child's need to have two parents is a set up for a lifetime of misery and self-doubt, you bad single mommy!

Sara is a single mommy of a ten-year-old child. "Every moment of every waking day is taken up by me doing—always doing—something." Sara works all day, then rushes (often late) to daycare, to rush home to eat dinner, to rush to bathe, to rush to bed, to rush to sleep. It's not playtime when she is parenting, it's "functional, rote work." Sara feels that there is so much parenting she has to do all by herself that it leaves her with no room for silliness. Being a single mommy is "very lonely. If it's just the two of you...it's not fun." Sara feels she is never "off"; the buck starts and ends with her.

Many of her friends are stay-at-home moms who enjoy whining about how hard done by they are in their pampered lives. It's hard for Sara to hear these complaints and "not be cynical." She wishes for a moment that they knew what her life is like. She's doing it all, and she is constantly judged. As a single, her love life is fertile grounds for discussion and amusement. Couple friends insinuate that she has been single too long because she is "too picky" and love to give her advice on finding a permanent mate. If and when she finds "Mr. Right," Sara is certain that he, their relationship, her timing of his introduction to her child, and any other action she takes or does not take will be arrogantly dissected by her self-satisfied married friends.

Keira is a fifty-year-old, thrice-married, often-single mother to two young adults. Keira was married young and "didn't know any single mothers. It just wasn't done in our social network." The feminist movement was gaining more and more momentum and started to enter her consciousness: "I was right on the tipping point of the change." Keira remembers hearing the song "One Less Bell To Answer" ("One less bell to answer, one less egg to fry") and realizing that her marriage to her children's father was over. "I was like, 'Fuck off, just leave. I'm not frying that egg for you.'"

At the time, Keira had "no remorse, no fear, no nothing," but in retrospect she says "we all ended up paying the price for my freedom." Her ex-husband opted out of supporting his children both financially or emotionally. A young single mother of two girls, Keira found herself with few options: "let's face it, I was a baby mother." Her parents were also "horrified, of course," as Keira's divorce was a first for the family. Keira married again a few years later. This was a "huge mistake, and done totally out of desperation." Keira was "screwed financially and out of my depth." Luckily, this husband didn't last long and the "third time was the charm." Her third husband was hand-picked by her daughters and "everyone likes him."

Ultimately, Keira is happy with her decision to become a single parent: "the girls were always my responsibility whether or not I was in a relationship." Her girls made Keira cards on Father's Day: "We just made a big funny out of it." Keira walked her daughter down the aisle at her wedding. "A mom's got to do what a mom's got to do."

Chapter 4

Bad Mommy Gets Knocked Up

Being a bad mommy starts even before the conception of your first child. Each pregnancy *should* be thoughtfully planned and considered, and at least three months of preparing the uterine nest and environment ought to occur before even considering using one's endometrium for work rather than play.

For example, folic acid is one of the most important substances a pregnant woman needs to have in her system to avoid wretched birth defects such as spina bifida. However, in order to perform this function, folic acid needs to be in the system before conception. Most of us do not have a diet rich in folic acid (most of us have no idea what folic acid is, let's be real), thus most women have already become bad mommies preconception with the shocking and neglectful lack of folic acid in our systems.

See how easy it is to be a bad mommy? It just takes baby steps!

If, by some miracle or due to her natural love for green leafy vegetables, Mommy-to-Be has had a preconception diet rich in folic acid, there are still many opportunities for her to hone her skills as a bad mommy.

Alcohol and pregnancy are each other's worst enemy. About 75 percent of our population drinks alcohol. About 25 percent of pregnancies are planned. This means that at least half of all pregnancies occur in people who do not know they are pregnant and who drink alcohol. In that first month before you know you are pregnant, use of alcohol can permanently damage your baby. Days 18, 19, and 20 of a pregnancy—before you have even missed your period—are responsible for the creation of most of the brain and the face. Who knows they are pregnant on days 18, 19, and 20?

The sad truth is that no amount of alcohol is safe, and most mothers drink some alcohol before they know they are pregnant. A mommy who drinks while she is pregnant, even if she does not know she is pregnant, is a bad mommy. Of course, since many children are conceived through the liberal assistance of alcohol, one can see how this is a bit of a Catch-22.

Once we see that double line on the pregnancy test, the majority of mommies know to lay off the sauce. However, the damage has probably already been done. Many women will still have a beer or glass of wine during pregnancy, and some women even report having health professionals who will admit that moderate use of alcohol in pregnancy is not harmful. Are you really going to trust these "health professionals"? They are not the ones stuck with the alcohol-damaged child for the next nineteen years, you are, Bad Mommy.

Don't think you can juice up guilt-free after your baby is born either. Alcohol passes through breast milk—of course, like nature would cut Mommy some slack—causing further damage to your young baby. Most bad mommies start to rely on that 3 p.m. martini or glass of wine pretty quickly after the birth of their children. After a night of no sleep followed by a lonesome, hollow day filled with self-abnegation, there is nothing like a big slug of vodka to make you feel better.

All you teetotalling mommies, stop feeling so smug. You can still fail at pregnancy by your unhealthy eating habits. If you eat fish during pregnancy, you are selfishly exposing the baby to harmful toxins, such as mercury found in tuna, which will likely give your unborn baby some terrible form of brain damage.

Should you think you are virtuous by eating sushi, think again. The parasites and toxins in raw fish will send you straight to mommy purgatory. Soft cheeses, such as brie and Camembert, are also forbidden pleasures. Soft cheeses are not pasteurized and likely contain harmful bacteria that will cause permanent brain damage to your child, you bad, exotic-cheese-eating mommy, you!

Why don't you just have a ham sandwich? Wait,

you can't do that either! Deli meats also contain harmful fetal toxins, you zygote neglector!

Love your cats? Great. Better not change their poo-box for the next nine months. The toxoplasmosis lurking in their poo-falafels will travel up your gravid bloodstream, permanently damaging your unborn charge.

Want to paint the baby's room before baby is born? Just another opportunity for more fetal harm! The old paint you are covering is probably full of lead, and just the act of painting it will cause latent flakes of lead paint to enter your blood system, causing permanent damage to your baby through lead poisoning. The new paint you are using in poorly ventilated space will enter your lungs and also cause unknown permanent damage. The simple act of preparing for your child's arrival will show you how easy it is to be bad.

Truly nothing Mommy can do during pregnancy is safe. If she drives, her seatbelt will be incorrectly positioned. The airbag could deploy, crushing and killing the unborn baby. If she has dental work done, she will disturb the mercury in her fillings, allowing it to enter her bloodstream and poison her developing child. As well, any x-rays done while pregnant will cause some horrible deformity down the road. Do you really think that lead apron does any good? Why do you think the x-ray technician leaves the room to push the button?

The only good pregnant mommy lives in a hermetically sealed environment, but you already know what kind of mommy you are. When you are pregnant, you become public property, and just about everyone has an opinion about how you are doing things wrong.

Kitty, age twenty-seven, is currently twenty-eight weeks pregnant with her third child. "With my first, it was all by the book, traditional pregnancy and parenting; with my second, it was all natural; and with this one, it's like I've completely forgotten I'm pregnant." Kitty doesn't have the luxury or the will power to say no to all those things good mommies say no to during pregnancy. "The only thing I've given up is the gin. I drink coffee. I go into Starbucks and they automatically ask if it's a decaf. I say no just to spite them." Kitty has moved furniture and painted her basement this pregnancy. "This time I do know what to expect when I'm expecting."

Kitty resents the fact that the pregnant are expected to live in a bubble. "I didn't want this pregnancy; it's hard to wrap my head around it. I'm not being a good mommy, and I don't really want to be a mommy to this baby at all." People are shocked by her continued lack of joy at being pregnant. At some point, she is expected to be happy. Kitty can't be really honest. She can't say how unhappy she is and that she doesn't want this baby. Kitty is trapped. "I had just started feeling like a grown-up—I could get a job—all that was going to start to happen, but now I'm pregnant."

Sally is finding herself contending with her AMA (Advanced Maternal Age) this pregnancy, as she is pregnant at age forty with her second child. She was recently seen by a doctor who expressed some concern with her age. This concern grew to alarm when she mentioned that her husband is in his late fifties. After a semi-lecture detailing the extensive list of nasty tests awaiting her due to her AMA, Sally was terrified: "Now I'm paranoid." The doctor encouraged her to read a massive pile of literature about the inherent risks of each test ranging from the "spontaneous abortion" of a healthy child, to the ominous and intriguing "damage to the limbs of the fetus."

This pregnancy, Sally reports feeling "really exhausted" and is finding "nothing interesting to eat." She says, "I have had this shit taste in my mouth for weeks; nothing works. I'm really fucking tired. I have no energy. I don't even have energy to go shopping." Pregnancy is no picnic in the park for her husband either: "There's no way that he can touch me. All my clothes are really tight and uncomfortable. I wake up in the middle of the night and I'm fucking nauseous. What is that? Does it not sleep?"

Chapter 5

Bad Mommy Gains Weight

Let us consider the case of weight gain in pregnancy. Women, fat, and body issues are never a pleasant combination. For any woman who has ever struggled with her weight, pregnancy and the postpartum period can be a lethal time.

The experience of being weighed monthly is a humbling one for the new Bad Mommy. Climbing up on the scale for each prenatal visit, seeing the nurse with your chart in one hand and her eyes widening imperceptibly as she notes your weight gain, and hearing the ever-so-subtle tsk in the doctor's voice as he (what is it with male gynecologists anyway?) chastens you for your burgeoning size will all add to the joy and acceptance of your expanding girth. Everyone knows that gaining too much weight is bad for you and the baby, not to mention your poor husband, you bad mommy!

Of course, only a month earlier many mommies-to-be are lectured to for losing weight. Constant vomiting and the refusal to eat anything with an odour during the first trimester makes many women actually lose weight for the first month or so. It's not uncommon for your gaunt cheeks to lull you into a false sense of safety through the pukey months. Nothing causes comments like a too-skinny pregnant woman. What a bad mommy: not lining her nest for baby; too concerned about her own appearance!

However, the weight loss tide quickly turns as we enter the second trimester and the feelings of nausea subside. Mommy-to-Be is gripped with a deep-seated hunger that is rarely satisfied, similar to a bear preparing for hibernation. With this stage of pregnancy, many of our old food "rules" go out the door. A former vegetarian will dream of pork ribs. A closet calorie counter will stock up on Ben & Jerry's ice cream—full fat! The second trimester almost makes up for the horrors of the first. Bad Mommy will use this trimester as an excuse to fulfill her most naughty hidden food desires. She will focus on the phrase "eating for two," losing sight of the fact that pregnancy really means eating for 1.2.

Doctors are fascinated by both the weight gain and the pee of expectant mommies. They will request samples of mommy-to-be pee at alarmingly regular intervals. As your weight goes up (and up and up), the doctor will closely examine your little pee strips for signs of sugar or other traces of minerals in order to show how inadequately you are managing your pregnancy. Should your pee show any signs of sugar or mineral spillage, you will be verbally reprimanded (and a note made on you chart) for your lack of control and care. You may be threatened with the diagnosis of the dreaded gestational diabetes or—horror of horrors—bed rest (always good for weight loss) if you do not clean up your pee strips quickly. Bad mommies with inappropriate pee strips will be sent to a special hospital detention room while they ruminate over the poor food choices they made in the preceding weeks of pregnancy.

Should you somehow manage to dodge the above problems, you may still be faced with one of the deepest horrors of pregnancy: stretch marks. Your stomach skin may start to split over the pressure of your burgeoning girth, covering your abdomen with red angry lines. Good mommies and their partners will have softened the stomach skin nightly with cocoa butter rubs, leaving no trace of the pregnancy. Slovenly bad mommies and their evil partners can be easily diagnosed by the presence of these lovely "badges of honour."

Giving birth does not solve any of these belly problems; instead of a massive taut belly, you now have a massive jelly-belly. Your breasts swell to a gargantuan size, making you closely consider the sanity of anyone who would consider getting breast implants. No clothes will fit, and you might have to suffer the indignity of staying in maternity clothes for months (years) postpartum. You are now not only bad, but HOT.

Many mommies feel the only option at this point is a crash diet, but that's not allowed for breastfeeding mommies either. Apparently, as you melt away the fat, all the toxins stored in that fat pour out of your breasts into your baby, who becomes a sort of lactation toxic waste dump. Unless you are a truly bad mommy, the only option available to you is to wait until your child is weaned to begin the reducing process.

Christine, a thirty-three-year-old mommy, knows the personal joy of weight gain in pregnancy. Upon learning that she was pregnant, Christine thought, "Fucking rock on! I can eat and I don't have to feel guilty." A casual eater before pregnancy, Christine found herself gripped with an intense need for calories. "I would get up first thing in the morning and think, 'Oh my God, I have to eat and I have to eat right now!'" During her first pregnancy, she gained sixty pounds in total, all to produce a seven-pound, twelve-ounce baby. Her doctor was "on her" by month four to stop gaining so much weight. "Each month it was try this, no try this, and each month it was another ten pounds."

Christine's situation was exacerbated by the diagnosis of placenta previa, or a low-lying placenta. The cure for placenta previa? No exercise for nine months! (And Christine's doctor couldn't figure out why she was gaining weight. Please!) Christine was truly a victim of pregnancy food cravings. She recalls eating a half-dozen hard-boiled eggs for breakfast one morning and dill pickle popcorn with peaches another. "I was hungry, and I ate when I was hungry."

Clara, a forty-one-year-old mother of two daughters, was in the enviable position of not gaining enough weight in pregnancy despite a deep-seated hunger and inhalation of anything not bolted down. By the fifth month of pregnancy, she had still not gained weight. Her doctor expressed increasing concern over her proper lack of weight gain and instructed her to "drink milkshakes"... since everyone knows the nourishment found in cow's milk and sugar is just what a developing fetus needs most!

Clara took these instructions to heart. Shortly afterwards, her body became totally swollen on an airplane flight. As the dreaded pregnancy edema set in, she gained almost forty pounds of water weight in four weeks. Even her fingers and eyelids were swollen. Once chastised for being too small, Clara was put on a diet and threatened with bed rest.

Chapter 6

Bad Mommy Gives Birth

Your utter failure as a mommy continues its journey through gestation and into the act of bringing your blessed darling into this world and your choice of location for this event.

In the olden days, it was rather simple. Mommy would work up until she was ten centimetres dilated, and then she would squat in a field, have her baby, and continue working. As we became more "civilized," mommies moved to having their babies at home with the help of a wise woman or midwife. Then, as a collective society, we decided that babies should be born in hospitals, preferably with the mommy unconscious (which honestly does have some appeal to many a bad mommy). Of course, the pendulum has started to swing back again and, slowly, hospital births are losing their appeal and home births are coming back into fashion. Never fear, whatever choices you make, there are ample bad feelings and guilt for all to share.

Hospital births are a harrowing and traumatic experience for many a mommy. Once you have that hospital band slapped on your wrist, you cease to be a human being: you have now become a patient. You cease to "do" and you now have things (horrible things) done to you. Luckily, the automatic enema and gratis Brazilian seem to have gone the way of the dodo, but there is still plenty to fret about with a hospital birth.

Your nether regions become public property in a hospital birth. You may have no less than thirteen sets of hands up your private bits to "check" on your progress. It is worse than a Roman orgy! As well, many hospitals are "teaching hospitals," meaning that at any point in your labour, a cast of twenty or so student doctors could enter the room for a little peek at your progress. With any luck, you may see a familiar face in the crowd, perhaps a high school sweetie or other long lost friend. Giving birth in a teaching hospital is a great way to meet all of the people in your city up close and personal.

Unless you are able to have a silent and pain-free birth (low moans only) à la TomKat in a Scientology Centre, you will most likely be offered a buffet of painkillers at the hospital. (This along with the lack of clean up afterwards is the saving grace of a hospital birth.) However, please note that taking any of these offered agents will make you a bad mommy! Any substance that you ingest will make its way into your baby, causing him or her to be "floppy" and have—*gasp*—a less than perfect Apgar score at birth. Bad mommies strive to get their babies high even before they make it out of the birth canal!

A common choice of painkiller for the labouring mommy is a combination of Demerol and Gravol, which is administered as a shot to your ass. You will immediately feel like vomiting and laughing your head off. Yes, you are being ripped in half, isn't that funny? Laughing gas is also a universal option, though it is a somewhat useless drug. It makes you feel like you have a bad hangover and causes the labouring mommy to make loud Darth Vader breathing sounds, and results in an unpleasant feeling of being only light-headed, yet still in pain. The epidural is considered by many to be the Holy Grail of birthing pain analgesics. At the point where Mommy is begging for the doctors to kill her and take the baby, this may be offered. Bad Mommy will first have to sign a release saying that if she is paralyzed forever or dies because of the lumbar puncture going badly, she will not sue the hospital. (Of course, she is under no duress while signing and completely in her right mind.) The added bonus of an epidural is the dreaded "spinal headache," a twenty-four- to forty-eight-hour headache of massive proportions that many women get the next day. There is something about puncturing your lumbar that just wreaks havoc on the old head. Early punishment for a bad mommy!

For many women, the epidural does help get through the pain. However, for an equally large number of women, the epidural slows the labour, causing further complications that often necessitate a Caesarean. Bad mommies who have a Caesarean will never experience the joy and perfection of having their vaginas flayed wide open. If you deny your baby and your body the experience of a beautiful vaginal birth, you are well on your way to being a bad mommy.

Although your Caesarean-born baby will have a lovely, rounded head (unlike those nasty vaginal babies and their funny cone heads), baby will not have experienced the squeezing of the birth canal and will most likely have lung problems as a result of not having their lung fluids squeezed out your vagina— the lung-squeezing method of choice of all good mommies! Further to this, you will have a sexy scar on your belly that will accentuate the seventy pounds you gained to give birth to a seven-pound baby.

Even the actual act of birthing separates the mommy wheat from the mommy chaff. Good mommies hold back from pushing when the doctor instructs them to pause. She quietly makes the sound of "blowing on soup," as she was taught in Lamaze classes, and the baby slowly emerges from her intact perineum. Bad mommies are selfishly interested in putting an end to the "ring of fire," as the baby's massive head actually stretches her in half. She bears down on the wee beastie between her legs, shooting it out watermelon-seed like, causing ripping, tearing, and other sundry damage. One can almost calibrate a mommy's badness by the number of stitches needed in her nether regions post-birth.

Of course, tides could turn and Mommy-to-Be could decide to be retro and have a "home birth." Midwives, doulas, and Birthing From Within are cooler than iPads with the generation "XYZ" set. Home births have all the joys of childbirth with the added bonus of no painkillers! Midwives are trained birthing professionals, but they are not allowed to administer pain relief in a home birth. The home birth is appealing from the whole "avoiding the commute to the hospital" angle. However, should anything go wrong at a home birth (very likely), you are looking at a scary evacuation to the hospital with the baby hanging half-way out of your bits as you manoeuvre the freeway at breakneck speeds.

All sorts of nasty things can and do happen during birth. Birthing killed many generations of mommies before us and is rife with strange hemorrhages, blood problems, and others mysterious issues of the womb. Babies get stuck, can't breath, and have racing hearts. Should anything go wrong at a home birth of your choice, welcome to the club: you are now a bad mommy, and no amount of incense, birthing pools, and Sarah McLachlan playing in the background can erase that fact.

Kathleen, a forty-one-year-old mommy, had a planned hospital birth for her child. She wanted it "as natural as possible" but was open to interventions, if necessary. Kathleen's labour stopped progressing after several hours. "I took the gas," she admits. Kathleen recalls a nurse telling her to stop pushing. "I'm not pushing. That would be my uterus," replied Kathleen. "You are going to tear your cervix!" the nurse said. Horrified by the notion, Kathleen accepted a spinal, the next intervention in line. "I was happily numb. 'Did you feel that?' they would ask. 'Did I feel what?'" With the spinal freezing, Kathleen couldn't feel or do anything. Eventually, the medical team realized that a C-section was needed, "I was a bit teary with feelings of inadequacy, but OK, whatever, let's just get it out," said Kathleen.

The real problems started after the birth. Kathleen recalls hearing, "We need to ask dad and baby to leave the room," followed by the horrifying, "I can't find anything resembling a cervix," and the terrifying, "It's like trying to sew up tissue paper." There was a tense moment when it appeared that two sponges were missing, perhaps inside her. Kathleen recalls them digging away inside of her abdomen, pushing her traumatized insides around to look for sponges that were eventually found in the garbage. In the end, Kathleen lost 50 percent of her blood but did live to tell the story.

Sara, aged forty-one, is a true believer in natural living. When her midwife asked what her plans were for her placenta post-birth, Sara was open to suggestions. Her midwife supplied her with a many-times-over photocopied recipe for powdered placenta. Apparently, eating one's placenta can be an excellent cure for postpartum depression.

To prepare the placenta, Sara had to cut it into thin strips and place it in her oven on cookie sheets at a low temperature. Sara shared that it is a similar technique to making beef jerky (no seasoning required!). The flesh took almost all day to dry out. It was unbearably nasty. "The placenta smell was everywhere." The horrifying burnt human organ odour passed upstairs through their shared house, causing their upstairs neighbours to complain in repulsion about the odour (to which Sara proclaimed innocence).

After it was dried, the next step was to pulverize the placenta with a coffee grinder before putting it into gelatin capsules. Sara only pulverized a small amount of placenta the first night. The next morning, she was forced to tell her horrified husband the composition of the claylike mess in the bottom of his coffee cup. Sara, a vegetarian, gave up after three days of eating her placenta pills. "I'm a self-cannibal. I had to stop. It was getting too weird."

Chapter 7

Bad Mommy and Her Boobies

Breastfeeding looks so easy, doesn't it? Baby Jesus was lifted to Mary's breast with a big smile and exposed palate. A good latch was achieved with no hassle; nipples were intact with a good let-down and flow. All is calm; all is bright.

Shockingly, babies don't actually come into this world knowing how to nurse. First-time mommies also do not know how to nurse a baby. Hence the whole scenario is kind of like two virgins fumbling in the back seat together for their first time: painful and embarrassing.

"Breast is best"— everyone seems to agree with this tenant of parenting. All good mommies must breastfeed. Breast milk is best for baby and best for Mommy, and, most important, for her hormones and body. However, the actual "art" of breastfeeding is much more challenging than meets the eye.

First, there is the all-important latch. In order for nursing to work, the latch has to be perfect. Remember, babies have no idea what they are doing. If their little mouth is somehow on your nipple incorrectly, they are still going to get their milk. It's Mommy who is going to pay. Any slight problem in positioning can and will lead to a plethora of nursing injuries including but not limited to: cracked and bleeding nipples, infection of the breast, and—God help us— mastitis (a.k.a. massive tit-is), a horribly painful condition sweetly known as "milk fever," where Mommy feels like dying while her huge throbbing boob looks angry and red and is about to explode with infected milk.

Good mommies "nurse through" the pain and 105 degree fevers, perhaps applying a poultice of warm cabbage leaves to the offending breast to help draw out the infection while baby happily nurses out the infected pus, blood, and milk. Charming. Bad mommies will run to the doctor for antibiotics that will be passed through the breast milk and give their babies bad teeth (see Bad Dental Care Mommy).

If she actually makes it through the latch and past mastitis and other sundry breast infections, a mommy is hardly out of the woods. Just because you can nurse, doesn't mean that you can do it. Nursing mommies need to feed their babies, well, all the time, anywhere. Despite our forward-seeming society, the nasty and incredulous looks faced by mommies willing to haul out their breasts in public are astounding. People may suggest you use a blanket or "nursing shawl" to afford privacy and keep the offending bosom out of the public eye, like a good little mommy. People who suggest this are clearly insane. How is Mommy supposed to see her baby to make sure they have a correct latch and are not ripping her boobs off under a blanket?

As well, once your baby is past three months of age, the whole "nurse passively" notion is out the window. They are little showboats, who will flash your booby for all to see: "Wee, I'm nursing! Wee, here is Mommy's booby! Wee, see how I twiddle her other nipple with my free hand?" Any mommy who retains (miraculously) a shred of decorum after giving birth will soon lose it through multiple public breast bearings. Nursing a baby is a public-private partnership with an impossibly public partner.

Even if you have nicely established breastfeeding, guilt about being a bad mommy is still only a thought away. A nursing mother's nutritional intake is fertile grounds for misgivings and fear. If the baby is gassy, Mommy had too much cabbage/chocolate/dairy/wheat/beans/whatever before nursing. The more you like something, the more likely it is that it will be the very substance that will forever curse your child through repeated breast-milk exposures. Never fear! If the baby is sleepy, it was that beer you drank! If the baby is rashy, Bad Mommy ate strawberries! God forbid you eat anything during nursing that might cause an allergy in baby later on in life. Bad mommies eat peanuts, shellfish, and soy and curse their poor nurslings to a lifetime of misery and allergies via toxic booby-milk exposure.

Then we come to the issue of weaning. In North America, most mommies wean before the age of one. The World Health Organization (WHO) suggests age two as a minimum for weaning; hence, all mommies who wean before the age of two are, by definition, "bad." Isn't it easy! Isn't it easy to be bad?

Never fear! Should you choose to wean past age two, you are still bad. Certain insane, yet good, mommies believe and espouse the notion of "child-led weaning." Child-led weaning means allowing your child to stop nursing when they are ready, whether this is at age two, five, eight, or sixteen. According to those who believe in this, the only good mommy is a mommy who never says no to nursing. Never.

Of course, women who breastfeed past the age of three or four are generally considered bad mommies as well. By never hearing "no" from Mommy, their children will fail to develop a good sense of boundaries and will end up with oral fixations, such as cigarette smoking or nail biting, in adulthood. Bad Mommy!

Tandem nursers are a subtype of nursing-saint: mommies who will nurse multiple children simultaneously and nurse through pregnancy. In true child-led weaning, nothing gets in the way of nursing. Some mommies will have multiple "nurslings" at a time. Don't you fret: these women are bad mommies too. They are stretched too thin and "aren't taking enough time for themselves," which will eventually result in hatred of their children and life itself. They are also leaching their bones and teeth of calcium from their incessant lactation and will be toothless with osteoporosis at a young age. They will develop dowager humps and brittle bones and be cursing their children to a lifetime of supporting fragile, toothless bad mommies, old before their time.

Sara, a forty-one-year-old mother of a ten-year-old daughter, is a firm believer in extended breastfeeding. Before giving birth, she envisioned herself nursing her baby for as long as two years. She really didn't see it going past her child being an infant. Much to her surprise, her baby didn't take instantly to nursing; there were typical problems with an incorrect latch and positioning. Perseverance and commitment to nursing paid off, and six days after birth, she started nursing well. Very, very well. Sara's daughter nursed incessantly.

Sara became a "human soother," as her daughter would nurse virtually all the time, whether she was awake or asleep. "I was nursing this thing constantly; I was in this nursing daze." Sara would always nurse, even while eating dinner, hunched over a nursing child, furtively grabbing a few bites. As her daughter grew older, she still loved nursing and showed no signs of wanting to self-wean.

Sara recalls nursing her then three-year-old preschooler in the cubby area behind her classroom after a long day of work. Her daughter's lanky long legs stretched out into the shoe area. As kindergarten approached, Sara felt she had to wean her child. "I couldn't see sending her to kindergarten still nursing." She eventually weaned her daughter "cold turkey" and still misses the convenience and power of the booby. It was the ultimate anti-tantrum device: any tantrum could be quickly averted with the addition of a Mommy-beverage.

Before giving birth, Christine, a thirty-three-year-old mommy of two, was "totally keen to breastfeed." The first night in the hospital, nursing seemed to go well, but by the second night, it was obvious to all that there was something wrong. Her baby "screamed and screamed and screamed," and the other mommies in the ward eventually complained. Christine wanted to feed her baby, but she was not producing milk. The "nipple-confusion-obsessed women" on the ward wouldn't allow her to give the baby a bottle and instead had her feed the baby formula in a cup—a cup! "They were doling formula out like it was co-caine: 'Oh no, you don't want to give her too much. Oh no, no, you can't use a bottle!'"

The next two months at home were torture. According to Christine, she was "nursing constantly, my nipples were cut and bleeding with blood actually coming out of my nipples. You feel so abnormal." Christine was sent to see a "lactation consultant" and put on special "milk-producing medication," but still, not enough milk was coming out. Christine was so desperate to nurse that when the doctor suggested they snip the bottom of the baby's tongue to see if that would help, she agreed. It didn't make a difference.

Christine finally admitted to herself and her doctor that "nursing is hell," and eight weeks after her daughter's birth, she conceded defeat. Shortly afterwards, an old woman approached Christine in the park while she was bottle-feeding her baby. She walked up and actually touched Christine's breast, shook her head, and said in broken English, "Why no breast? No bottle!" "You've got to be fucking kidding me," said Christine. "I felt terrible all day. It's not only the guilt from the social pressure, I felt inadequate that my body wasn't doing what a woman's body should do."

Chapter 8

Bad Mommy Names Her Child

They say—and "they" are always right, aren't they?—that there is only one chance to make a first impression. This all-important impression of a person is made when we hear their name for the first time. Names are an important and integral part of our identity, yet we have little to no control over our own names. The lovely moniker that shapes and follows us around for most of our lives was most often given to us by our mommy.

Naming someone is an intimate act, and most mommies will give this a great deal of thought. The proposed name for their neonate will likely have historical or family roots, or will at the very least derive from a popular soap opera.

Oh, the ways we torture our children with their names! If Mommy elects for a simple and "proven" name, her child will never feel special or cherished. Bad Mommy obviously knew at birth that her child would live a colourless, background sort of life, and thus she named him something boring that no one will ever be able to recall. Sure, everyone can spell and pronounce *Jessica* and *Jason*, but who cares? No one will ever remember them in the first place.

There are no truly "safe" names. Even the most innocuous can inspire hatred from someone who once knew someone with that name who was horrible. Most people will feel compelled to share their hatred with a potential name and the historic roots of this distain to a pregnant mommy foolish enough to publicly ruminate on a name for her unborn baby. It is virtually impossible to locate a negative-connotation-free name.

Some bad mommies try to give their child's name a slight tweak by giving their "safe" name an original spelling. Not only is little Lyndah now cursed with a name that no one will ever remember, now no one will ever spell it correctly either, which is the only redeeming quality of the safe name.

Other mommies look for a contemporary name for their young—something new and fresh that has been in the news or on TV lately. There will be a predominance of the same name in each grade in a school, which will reflect the TV lineup of the previous decade. By striving to give her child a fresh-sounding name, Bad Mommy will curse her child by forever dating them and never allowing them the anonymity of a name not tied into popular culture.

Some bad mommies choose to go with a truly unique name, often inspired by nature, such as Apple, Sequoia, or Willow. These mommies are drug-addled hippies obviously suffering from left-over flashbacks from the sixties. How can a CEO of a company be called Rainbow? People, think about it! While these whimsical nature names are cute on a baby, someday little Starfish is going to grow up and will need a serious name. As well, people will assume some mystical connection between your child and the nature object for which they have been named. The expectation that your child has some mysterious connection with a plant or mineral is unfair and will result in untold hours of psychotherapy in your child's adult years.

The worst of all mommies will consider naming her child after a family member—bonus marks for a parent! It's such a good idea to have two people in the house with the exact same name! Naming your child after yourself or your partner is a surefire way to ensure that Junior never forms their own identity, and instead stultifies under your staggering name and expectations from the earliest of ages.

The pressure to come up with the perfect name is so great that some mommies cannot deal with it. More and more are waiting the allotted thirty days to name their child, which makes shower gifts and phone calls to check on "Little Baby No Name" all the more interesting. As day 30 approaches, the desperate mommy is inundated by well-wishers who have a great deal of anxiety over her unnamed child. By the time the child is finally named, it is too late.

"Little Baby No Name" will not have had the early connection to their name and will forever respond to the concept of "No Name," cursing them to a lifetime of thrift shopping and a lack of well-formed ego identity. Bad Mommy!

Lilah, aged thirty-seven and mother to one son aged two, has had "life-long strong opinions about names." When she discovered she was having a boy (a clever trick which really does narrow down the field of choices), she realized that she had only chosen girl names. Since she and her partner are both English professors, they wanted a "literary name," such as Wordsworth or Tennyson, but nothing seemed to fit. At one point she wanted to name her child Oliver, middle name Vernon, but then she realized, to her chagrin, that those were two small towns in the interior of British Columbia. "I couldn't do that. What would people think?" Eventually, they hit upon the author Dashiell Hammett, and the perfect literary and original name "Dashiell."

Two months after the birth of little Dash, Lilah's cruel sister phoned to inform her (with some amount of glee) that a major blockbuster movie *The Incredibles* had just been released, and a main character in this animated flick about a "superhero family" was a little boy named Dashiell, or Dash for short. Why didn't she just name her child "Nemo" and get it over with? "Now everyone thinks I named my son after an animated cartoon character." Lilah also notes that as Dash goes through his two-year-old bolting phase and she chases him, yelling, "Dash! Dash!" it appears as though she is goading him on. Although older folks are generally horrified by her name choice, Lilah reports that the "mall girls love it."

Keira, a fifty-year-old mother of two young adults, has had "many people question me about my name choices for my girls." Her first daughter, Rebekka, was named after a character on a soap opera. "When I was pregnant with her, I was doing the traditional little housewife thing, and I loved that character. She was dark and beautiful." Keira's Rebekka grew up to be a lover of names and semantics, being named after a soap opera is a dark and somewhat shameful little secret. Rebekka was known as "Star" in utero, and Keira sometimes wishes she had kept that name. Some people reacted to her name choice, feeling "Rebekka" was "a little ethnic. We weren't Jewish or anything, just plain old WASPs. The name confused people."

Friends and family were thus not overly surprised when she named her second child "Cedar." "I wanted to name her Sandra after a friend, but my husband thought Cedar would be more 'far out,' so we went with that." At the time, Keira was beginning to live the "hippie" lifestyle, so Cedar fit right in. "But really," explains Keira, "it's not so bad. Everyone can spell it and pronounce it; that's something!" This combination of names wasn't accepted by all. Keira overheard her divorce lawyer say, "Well really, someone who names their children Rebekka and Cedar, what do you expect? Of course they are going to get a divorce!" Luckily, Keira moved to a hippie village soon after the divorce and found "my kids had the most normal names there."

Chapter 9

Bad Mommy's Dink Cutting Dilemma

Until the eighties, most mommies in North America had their little boys circumcised: it was a no-brainer. Whack off the end of little Johnny's wee-wee: end of discussion. Most of our partners, being born prior to the nineties, are likewise circumcised, so it seems normal. In fact, to many of us, an adult intact penis is rather shocking, it is such a rarity.

Well, it turns out that removing a part of someone's body is actually a bad idea. Studies have confirmed that little babies feel pain just as much as everyone else, and that the penis (surprise, surprise) has more nerve endings in it than just about any other place in the body. Even if a circumcision is done with pain control (not always the case), little boys who were circumcised have a stronger reaction to pain the day of the operation, the next day, a month later, ten years later. Basically, you have condemned your child to a lifelong extreme reaction to pain by creating such a strong pain response at such a young age, you bad circumcising mommy! This ongoing response to pain may cause your child to become a psychopath as an adult and go on killing sprees. This will be entirely your fault for removing his penis tip in infancy.

A common reason given for circumcision is that men want their little boys to "look like them" down there. This is such a bizarre concept. First of all, what kind of parent and child compare their genitals for familial similarities? "Well, sweetie, I think she has her Aunt June's labia." Pu-lease! Second, even if they are both cut, they aren't going to look the same anyway. Children generally do not have hairy genitals, and an adult reproductive system is generally much larger and baggier than a child's. Women and their daughters never sit around comparing vulvas. That's just nasty.

Pro-circ advocates call attention to studies showing that people who are circumcised have lower rates of cancer and lower rates of HIV and other sexually transmitted diseases. This may be the case, but who really knows why? It could be that those circumcised adults have less sex than intact ones. We really don't know what the cause is. Yes, circumcised penises are easier to clean, but I suppose vulvas with clitorectomies are easier to clean too. If you do this to your child, you are dooming them to a life of heightened pain response and the loss of sexual pleasure.

Men feel strongly about their penises, and it's a general rule of thumb not to go around desecrating something that people tend to worship. Recent court cases reported in the press have involved grown men suing doctors who circumcised them as infants without their consent. Support groups for men wanting to reclaim their lost foreskins abound. There are even techniques for stretching foreskins involving complicated weights attached to the penis. So-called "Intactivists" are lobbying governments to reform laws allowing circumcision. This penis issue is not going away.

Of course, in typical bad mommy fashion, should you not circumcise your child, you will undoubtedly be failing them as well. They will likely get a horrible sexually transmitted disease, since it has been proven that circumcised penises are less likely to attract nasties of the privates. They will suffer in permanent penile pain because of your lack of foresight on the foreskin issue. Even worse, your adult child may have to endure an adult circumcision due to some strange event such as a penile torsion or religious epiphany. The humiliation and pain of suffering an adult circumcision will once again be all your fault for not having the prescience to anticipate the need to rid your child's penis of its tip in infancy when the whole thing would have been forgotten in the fog in babyhood, you bad mommy!

The circumcision discussion first came up between twenty-seven-year-old Kitty and her husband when she was about four months pregnant with her first child. Her husband was circumcised, and his family was very pro-circ—not for any religious reason, they just "thought it looked better." He also had a friend at work who had needed a circumcision in his thirties, and the pain and humiliation his friend had suffered was making him lean towards the operation.

Kitty decided to wait until her child was born to see if it was an issue or not. When they lowered the sheet from her C-section to tell her "it's a boy," the first thought through her mind was: "Oh, shit. What are we going to do about the circ?" Everyone had an opinion about her child's penis. One cousin actually commented, "Look at all the porn. You never see an un-circed penis in porn." It was as though Kitty was robbing her child of a future in the adult entertainment industry through her selfish decision not to circumcise. Ultimately, the decision was made for financial reasons, not esthetics. It turns out that the family had to pay about $300 out-of-pocket for an infant circumcision, which was enough to push her husband over to the other side.

Christine, a thirty-three-year-old mommy of two, is extremely pleased that she is the mommy of two girls. The issue of circumcision has never found resolution in her family, and with each impending birth, she and her husband were not able to come to any happy conclusions. "My husband is circumcised, and in his family, that's just what you do. He thinks it would be weird if their penises [his and his sons'] looked different." Christine feels that's nonsense: "Not every vagina is created equal." She believes the real reason for circumcision is vanity: "It's cosmetic; they do it because it looks nicer." Before each birth, they attempted to settle this issue. "We did research. I would find articles and print them off and give them to him." Her husband was "not totally daft. He did worry about the medical aspects, like what if something went wrong in the procedure?" But it was his need to have his child circumcised, not the baby's.

When she went into labour, they were still at loggerheads. Christine finally conceded and let him make the decision. "Whatever he decided; he was responsible. He could make the appointment, he could take the baby there, he could hold it while it was done, and he could explain to our son why I was not going to be any part of it." She went on, "It's like female genital mutilation—we are all appalled when it's women, but not when it's boys. It's such a double standard."

Chapter 10

Bad Mommy Gets Her Beauty Sleep

There is something so beautiful about a sleeping baby...so calm, so serene, so quiet, um, so quiet.

Who would have suspected that baby sleep is an area rife with mommy guilt? Where, how, and why your baby sleeps is perhaps the most charged and confusing area of parenting and is guaranteed to saddle you with guilt no matter what direction you choose.

The biggest conundrum involves where baby sleeps. At this time, there are two much-divided camps on this issue. Many people feel that babies need to sleep in a crib in their own rooms. This allows baby to learn independence, i.e., that Mommy and Daddy will not meet their needs at night. This also allows Mommy and Daddy to have much-needed private time in bed to work on making younger siblings.

When we were babies, and still for many families in North America, crib sleeping was the norm. However, despite their darling bumper pads and soothing rounded corners, cribs are truly an instrument of the devil. Putting your baby to sleep in a crib teaches them early on that their parents (especially their bad mommy) are unavailable for them at night. In the evening, the baby is a second-class citizen. Bad mommies with crib babies will not allow a true attachment with their child if they do not offer twenty-four-hour solace within an arm's reach. Putting baby to sleep in a far-flung "cage"—bonus marks if they are in a separate room; double bonus marks for a room on another floor from Mommy!— is inhumane and something a bad mommy will do to please her husband's insatiable lust rather than meet the attachment needs of her young child.

For purely selfish reasons, cribs just don't make sense. If you are breastfeeding, would you actually want to get out of bed to feed the baby, burp baby, settle the baby back in its cage, and then stumble back to bed? How cold…how tedious.

On the other hand, your baby can sleep with you and your partner in bed, where they will have unfettered access to your boobies and love. This form of sleeping is known as "co-sleeping," "the family bed," or "birth control." Never fear! You will also be a bad mommy if you choose this option, as you will clearly blur appropriate boundaries with your child, creating an overly dependent monster who will never be able to go to Girl Guide camp or sleepovers because of her nighttime neurosis and unhealthy attachment to her mommy. Further to this, should you co-sleep, you will likely smother your wee baby with your girth and heavy sleeping due to drug and alcohol use and fat. (Periodic studies are released showing the occurrence of smothering deaths of babies by mommies (bad), usually correlated with mothers who are obese and/or sleeping too heavily because of substance use, which, of course, will happen to you, being the bad mommy that you are.)

Furthermore, if your child actually survives your bed, you will never have normal sexual relations with your partner again. There is something about having sleeping children and their accoutrement in your bed that just kills your libido. Your child will end up with confused sexual boundaries, will never leave your bed, and will never have normal relationships with peers. Your husband will start surfing the web for online porn, and your marriage will slowly dissolve, all because you selfishly wanted your child to bond with you at night, Bad Mommy.

Positioning your baby to sleep is likewise ripe grounds for showing your failure as a parent. Sleep positioning rules have changed no less than three times in the last ten years. First, babies were to sleep on their tummies so that vomit would spill out their darling little mouths and they would not choke to death. Then, no, that was terrible! Babies had to be propped on their sides so that vomit could drain out of their darling mouths with no choking. Of course, a year or so later, this changed again and all good mommies put their babies to sleep on their backs so that the vomit can drain out of their darling little mouths and they will not choke to death somehow (like babies actually stay in the position you put them to sleep in anyway). Babies not sleeping on their backs will likely get SIDS (sudden infant death syndrome) and die, the direct result of poor sleep positioning by their bad mommy. Likely by the time this book is published, babies will need to sleep suspended upside down from the left ankle only, which will allow for optimal vomit drainage.

Clara is a forty-one-year-old mother of two girls, aged eleven and eight. Her first child was a perfect sleeper. By five weeks of age, she was sleeping through the night and always woke up with a big smile on her face. Clara and her husband were lulled into a false sense of complacency. Her second child "came out screaming." She would sleep "from 7 p.m. to 11 p.m. That's it." Her "screaming started just after lunch and built from there." She was "born with a black cloud over her head and a knot in her chest." Clara and her family "walked on eggshells" when the baby was sleeping. Her child, now eight, often questions why there are so few baby pictures of her; Clara admits "there were so few opportunities when she wasn't screaming."

Prolonged sleep deprivation almost destroyed this mommy. She says, "I remember waking up—she was four weeks old—she kept going and going and going. It was four in the morning. I remember feeling like I was fading away, my body was paper-thin and I was fading away. There was nothing left. I just burst into tears, thinking, 'I'm not even human anymore.'" Clara recalls one occasion where she left the screaming baby in her crib while she went out to the porch to curse and kick and destroy all of her patio furniture to the background sound of her screaming child. "We would put the baby gate up at 10 p.m. and go to bed; we really didn't know when she went to bed or what she was up to." Eventually, she would run out of steam and pass out.

Sara, a forty-one-year-old mother of a ten-year-old daughter, was committed to extended breastfeeding and also getting some sleep herself, so co-sleeping (sleeping in the same bed as your child) seemed like the obvious answer. This co-sleeping arrangement worked well for Sara, a single mother at the time, and her daughter for several years. Sara enjoyed cuddling and nursing her daughter and didn't see any reason to have her child sleep elsewhere. However, by the time her child reached six years old, Sara was starting to feel the need for some privacy in her bed. She gently tried to move her daughter out of her bed at that time, but her daughter refused, stating, "I'm not ready for this; it's not working for me!" Sara abandoned this attempt and remains trapped in bed with her ten-year-old at night.

Sara is truly besieged. She can't watch TV with the sound on, read with a bright light, or, most important, "entertain." Co-sleeping has lost its charm as Sara's daughter enters pubescence. Sara is not quite sure how this is going to end. Her daughter sees her asking her to leave the bed as a personal rejection. "It's me not wanting her.... I don't know when it's going to end. I need professional help to help us break through."

Chapter 11

Bad Mommy Cries It Out

High-pitched crying was specifically designed to elicit a response in adults. Its noxious nature makes us desperate to stop it as quickly as possible. The natural response to a crying baby is to pick it up, soothe it, feed it, change its diaper, or do whatever types of strange swaying dance and murmuring is necessary to make it stop crying.

Of course, nothing is straightforward in mommying. Some people believe that reacting to your baby's cries will foster a dependence on the parents, and the child will not learn the all-important skill of soothing itself and accepting the fact that it is all alone and unloved in the world: the ultimate human state. This is particularly important at bedtime. Mommies who respond to their child's every cry for attention and love will only be setting up their child for a lifetime of codependent relationships and likely substance abuse, as these children will search for ways to replace their bad mommy's undying and ceaselessly focused attention when they are feeling down and lonesome as adults. Many feel it is kinder to teach this lesson at an early age: no one cares about you when it's nighttime.

In response to this, some mommies embrace attachment parenting. According to the theory of attachment parenting, by responding to your child's every desire, whimper, or notion, you are creating a secure and happy little person who will go on to conquer the world and discover the end to world hunger or make some equally deserving discovery due to their happy and secure sense of self.

Mommies who are snookered into believing this approach are actually doing the exact opposite. By responding fully to every crisis, big or small, real or imagined, these mommies are creating little monsters. Children raised in the attachment parenting paradigm expect adults to jump when they snap their little attached fingers. These tiny dictators can ruin a parent's life for decades because they will not sleep by themselves and have no idea of how to self-soothe. Every hangnail becomes a cellphone call to Mommy to come with her first aid kit. As adults, children raised expecting every whim to be answered will be nightmares as employees, lovers, and parents themselves. By teaching your child that they are soooo special, you will be setting them up for some big reality lessons in later life.

However, the other choice is not so perfect either. Many of us were raised in the good old "traditional," parent-centred Dr. Spock method of parenting that was recently re-championed by Dr. Ferber in his infamous *Solve Your Child's Sleep Problems* books.

Should you, a bad mommy, eschew attachment parenting and instead embrace this parent-centred method of child rearing, you will have children who sleep by themselves through the night. The parent-centred approach teaches the child who is boss: Mommy. However, by its dictatorial nature and spirit-crushing need for child conformity, the "parent-centred" approach will also be creating lifelong damage in your child.

Children need to form at least one attachment to at least one caregiver in their earliest days. Attachments are formed by reacting to a baby's cues, for example, crying. If you as a parent do not react to your baby's cry on demand, you will be teaching baby early on that no one cares for them and that no one can be trusted. As your child grows, this lesson will translate into anti-social personality disorder, and your child will become either a lawyer or mass murderer. Or both.

Many parents will let their babies "cry it out" so that the parents themselves can have peace at night. This is short-sighted, like drinking aspartame in your coffee; yes, there are no calories, but you will get cancer in the end. Children who are not "attached" to their parents, although excellent sleepers, do not really care what kind of havoc they are wreaking in their family home and later on in society.

No matter which method you adopt, you will be a bad mommy, so relax. With crying management and intensive parenting, it's "pay now or pay later." Either deal with comforting your crying baby and the clingy ramifications or wait until the tell-all book comes out from behind prison bars, detailing the neglectful and unloving childhood they had at your hands, Bad Mommy.

Bridget's first-born would never sleep. She breastfed twenty-four hours a day straight for the first six months. If she wasn't nursing, she was crying. Bridget would overhear other mommies in the park who were discussing children sleeping through the night—a mythical occurrence in her opinion—and she would think, "I'm going to kill everyone in this park." Her daughter would not sleep for more than four hours until she was almost three. Everyone had something to say about this. "If a baby doesn't sleep through the night, it is automatically Mommy's fault.... It's either you are coddling her, feeding her too much, or not enough, you have no routine. Whatever, it's Mommy's fault."

Eventually, Bridget stumbled across Dr. Richard Ferber and his book about "teaching" children to sleep through the night through a "crying it out" technique. According to Dr. Ferber, this teaching will take a week at most and will last forever. Bridget was desperate, so they started "sleep training." The screaming only got worse. She can recall standing outside her daughter's room, physically choking her husband as a result of being filled with insane rage caused by the incessant screaming.

Contrary to results promised by Dr. Ferber, their daughter did not take well to "sleep training" and the screaming went on and on and on, despite three different attempts to get her to "sleep through the night." They were living in an apartment building, and in the morning, Bridget found sticky notes on her door that read: "'We are being kept awake by your baby's crying.' Like I had all these choices! Like I was choosing to have a screaming baby! I was completely strung-out; I literally do not remember chunks of that time period."

Christine, a thirty-three-year-old mommy of two, almost succumbed to the allure of "crying it out." A good friend had Dr. Ferber's book on teaching your baby to sleep through the night and "swore by it." Every time Christine would get up to attend to her fussing baby, this friend would pressure her: "Why don't you just let her cry? Once they learn that you are ignoring them, the crying ceases." It was an appealing prospect on some levels. Christine admits to trying crying-it-out a couple of times. Alas, neither she nor her husband had the nerve to last through the crying sessions. Christine recalls putting the baby in her crib, then running to her own room to watch the clock for the allotted and dreaded ten minutes of screaming and thinking, "'How the fuck can anyone do this?' I was totally in distress waiting for the numbers to turn."

Dinnertime was another time of crying in Christine's home. Friends would say, "Just let her cry in another room while you eat your dinner." Christine really appreciated these thoughtful and useful suggestions from the peanut gallery: "Boy, that's a really an enjoyable dinner...with a baby screaming in the other room." Christine eventually conceded defeat: "We'd end up bringing her into our bed and she'd sleep with us."

Chapter 12

Bad Mommy Feeds Her Young

Once her young have reached the six-month mark without infanticide (miracles do happen!), Mommy must consider the introduction of solid foods. In the olden days, that being the mid-nineties, mommies were instructed to introduce solids at three months, beginning with simple rice cereal and slowly introducing veggies, fruits, and eventually meats. The bad mommies following this sage advice exposed their infants' immature and unprepared digestive tracts too early to the abuses of solid digestion, resulting in allergies, indigestion issues, colic, and likely lifelong food-based issues.

Doctors now tell mommies that the introduction of solids should occur no earlier than at six months of age. Of course, I hope mommies do not need to be reminded that this will change inevitably, so that whenever it is that you choose to introduce solids, it will be patently wrong.

Good mommies prepare their own baby food from organic produce that they have grown themselves or fair-traded with the local farmer for handicrafts. Good mommies know that commercial baby foods are composed of fillers and additives that will irreparably harm their young. A good mommy can be noted by her ever-present baby food mill to grind up organic food for baby and her handy bag of appropriate, organic beverages and snacks available twenty-four hours a day at one-second notice.

Bad mommies will purchase baby food from stores, perhaps not even organic! Bad Mommy will heat up her baby food in the microwave, even though she knows it kills some of the nutrients in the food. Bad Mommy will feed her baby fruits instead of veggies because that is what baby prefers to eat. Bad Mommy knows that ketchup counts as a vegetable and that a daily multivitamin will cover a multitude of sins.

Bad Mommy is rarely prepared with snacks on the go and can be found at a concession stand, purchasing a treat for her baby. If Bad Mommy ever does come prepared with a snack (unlikely), it will be filled with allergens, store-bought, and a potential choking hazard.

Eating with the family is an important part of the day. Good Mommy, baby, and Daddy sit around the dinner table, gazing into each other's eyes and discussing their days while they appreciate and slowly digest the feast laid out before them. Bad Mommy sticks some leftover macaroni in the microwave (bonus points if heated in Styrofoam or plastic that will release toxins into the food) and slaps it down in front of the TV so that baby will leave her alone while she hunkers down over some lukewarm leftovers, wondering when Daddy will get home so she can go and hide under her quilt with some chocolate.

Star, the thirty-four-year-old mother of an eleven-year-old girl, has failed for over a decade in her attempt to feed her child according to the needs of the outside world. Star's daughter basically "wouldn't eat anything up until age eight." Star was perpetually concerned that her child would waste away from malnutrition and recoiled from frequent comments such as "what's wrong with her? She's so little!" Star's own mother had anorexia, so Star was increasingly anxious about this lack of eating. When her daughter reached age eight, she started to eat a little more, but she still wouldn't eat "with the food touching." All food items had to be separated on a plate. Star's daughter won't eat sandwiches, so lunches at school are a constant source of anxiety. "I can't even look at the other mommies' lunches; if I see what they pack and what their children eat, I'll just die."

Star is also suffering mommy guilt over not feeding her child only organics. Her daughter has recently sprouted small breasts, and she has been told that it was likely her lack of organic cow's milk that has resulted in this early breast blooming. People look at her daughter's chest and they say, "It's all in the food." Star knows what they mean. The poisonous, non-organic, breast-creating cow hormones are in all the food that a Bad Mommy feeds her young.

Scarlett, a thirty-six-year-old mother of a ten-year-old boy and seven-year-old girl, had the best intentions with her children in terms of feeding and nourishing them. A trained chef and vegetarian, Scarlett was very aware of the importance of good wholesome foods. Although she went back to work early, it was only breast milk in a syringe for her son. Formula was forbidden and likened to "little pieces of Satan" running down his throat.

Scarlett quickly turned her pure-food tune. "All of a sudden, I started eating hot dogs all the time," she says. "I was a trained chef, but now all I eat is crap, bland boring food." Scarlett admits to using sugar to keep her family happy. Saturday morning it's "chocolate-frosted sugar bomb cereal in milk." After school it's a "carb hit of an enriched sugar cereal." Scarlett's family has cereal or cinnamon toast (with real icing sugar and butter!) every morning. To complicate issues, one of her children is a vegetarian and the other is a "total carnivore." Scarlett is basically a short-order cook.

Recently, someone mentioned to her that all the soy she has been giving her children is bad. Soy will "give your daughter cancer and your boy breasts. To think I was feeling so smug about soy!" Scarlett has admitted food defeat. "I'm probably fucking up," she sighs.

Chapter 13

Bad Diapering Mommy

As with all aspects of parenting, whatever choice we make will damn us to eternal parenting hell. The choices that we make in dealing with our little darlings' poopies and pee-pees are not exempt. The disposable diapers our parents were so happy to embrace have now been discarded as short-sighted, wasteful landfill-fillers.

Good mommies are embracing cloth once again, which is also rife with its own downsides. Remember, there was a reason our mothers before us dumped cloth for "sposies" (as disposable diapers are repugnantly referred to by a certain subset of diaper-obsessed mommies).

Disposable diapers are actually harmful to children! Besides permanently damaging your baby's karma through landfill waste, disposable diapers are filled with a gel-like substance that will undoubtedly give your baby cancer, infertility, or, at the very least, a diaper rash. As a fun experiment, fill up your bathtub with water. Place a disposable diaper in the tub, come back three hours later, and observe. The water will disappear completely, leaving a massive jelly sack of vaguely diaper-shaped goop in your tub. This fantastic feature will allow you to only change your baby when absolutely necessary (i.e., you encounter a big, stinky number two or a relative comes over for dinner).

You know there has to be a catch for such convenience, right? Careless, shallow bad mommies use disposables because they are only thinking of themselves and convenience. Furthermore, recent studies have shown that the great heat generated by the gel and urine combination found in a sposie actually heats little baby boys' balls and can potentially render him sterile as an adult, all because of your selfish desire for a dry bum.

The only bad-karma-reducing sposie on the market is a new line of biodegradable (meaning here "useless") sposie that won't last through the lightest of baby pees and will force you to change baby approximately once every thirty seconds, thereby completely undoing any so-called karma reduction. Only bad mommies use sposies.

If you want your child to go anywhere but hell in the afterlife or you ever want to have grandchildren should your baby be a boy, cloth diapers are your only option. Cloth, of course, is also problematic. Should you choose a cloth diaper delivery system, you will be harming the environment, as the trucks used to pick up the soiled diapers, not to mention the hot water and chemicals used to wash them, are damaging the environment at a great rate. As well, the women hired to clean your soiled diapers probably have PhDs in the Philippines and have given up their own families and dreams to come to North America to wash your child's nasty diapers. More karmic harm, Bad Mommy!

Should you choose to wash your own cloth, you will quickly realize why people use a diaper service. After more than a day of sitting in a wet bucket, dirty diapers will start to ferment like a psychotic fecal sourdough. Placing that turdy mixture into your own washing machine will forever bathe the rest of your family in E. coli bacteria that may lead to death or other unpleasantries such as dysentery, Bad Mommy!

Should you still feel the need to explore cloth diapers, be warned that this is not a world for the faint of heart. Cloth diapers, bizarrely, seem to have a hypnotic effect on some women who become obsessed with the world of cloth. These women refer to themselves as "diaper hyenas" (for reasons unknown) and can be observed giving up all other decent and normal vices such as alcohol and eBay to chase the dream of the perfect diaper "stash." I kid you not; these "hyenas" take pictures of their diaper collections and post them on the internet for others to appreciate. They do not do this in jest. A proper "stash" will include all natural fibres, preferably hemp and wool so that your baby's bottom smells like it's 4:20 on a lamb farm. These super diapers come with a high price tag. People pay over $50 for one single diaper, not to mention the organic, free-range, shade-grown, exploitation-free, bamboo matching cover.

Besides being strangely consumerist and status-grasping, cloth diapers have the added bonus of not actually working. Cloth-using parents quickly become used to damp patches wherever baby's bum has been. Cloth babies are perpetually moist and stinky. Sure, their karma might be better than a sposie baby, but who really wants to hold your squishy, pissy baby? Bad mommies who expose the rest of us to their damp offspring are bathing the world in the warm body fluids of their young, most likely starting some sort of vile epidemic only spread through baby urine.

In your career as a mommy, you may hear of an odd practice known as "elimination training." This means that baby never wears a diaper of any kind. Never. Never ever! In elimination training, the mommy and baby are so in tune and connected that Mommy reads baby's subliminal bathroom cues and pulls the baby out from its sling (temporarily interrupting nursing!) and hangs the baby's bottom over the ground where it does its business. With elimination training, a child can apparently be "trained" by age one. It is not clear when the parent would recover, if ever. This all sounds interesting in principle, depending on your tolerance of omnipresent wee-wee.

Should you, as an aspiring good mommy, be considering elimination training, I would love to congratulate you...at your house (or, possibly, an open field).

Diapers are evil, but at least they are somewhat hygienic.

Kitty, a twenty-seven-year-old mother of a six- and two-year-old and who is twenty-eight weeks pregnant with her third, has run through the diaper gamut. With her first, it was disposable diapers all the way. When the baby was fourteen months old, a hippie friend offered Kitty some cloth diapers, and eventually she switched over to cloth. People told her that once her son was in cloth, he would be toilet trained immediately, but Kitty would like it to be known that this was a load of shit (so to speak).

With her second Kitty was going to use cloth all the way. She even admits to owning an organic hemp diaper. However, her mom brought over a big bag of disposables in the first week and she succumbed to their ease of use. Kitty doesn't mind cloth, as long as it is understood that shitty diapers are not her responsibility. She leaves them in the toilet for "Daddy to deal with" when he comes home.

Kitty finds that the older "career moms" look down their noses at her cloth using, as they feel it is some kind of excessive political statement. She uses cloth not because of landfills or the planet or some higher cause, but because disposables are very expensive and she was facing two children in diapers. They can think what they want.

Olivia was initially "really enthusiastic" about using cloth and to this end even hired a diaper service to collect her child's soiled diapers. Olivia felt quite strongly about the correctness of her decision to use cloth and felt the need to share this with everyone: "I'd made all my friends feel guilty for using disposables. I was on the high and moral ground." The moral ground didn't last long. Once the charm of using cloth started to fade, Olivia faltered in her faith in cloth. "I gave up after two months; I felt like a big failure." Her cloth shame was only exacerbated by her prior public commitment to cloth.

Olivia attributes her cloth experience to the vast and sheer number of wet nappies with which she was assailed. She was shocked at the actual number of wet diapers her child created: "I had to change them every five minutes." Switching to disposables was not easy on her conscience though. "I had visions of landfills. I don't think they ever actually biodegrade, really ever, do they?" Despite her best intentions, Olivia just couldn't follow through with the tyranny of cloth diapers. "I was a pioneer in cloth. A failed pioneer."

Chapter 14

Bad Mommy Clothes Her Young

For many a burgeoning bad mommy, the first inkling of clothing-related failure occurs well before the birth of her first child. About eight months into pregnancy, someone is sure to enquire about preparations for the layette. Fearful of error, and unclear that such a construct in fact exists, she will consult a Mommy bible that explains that the layette is the suite of clothing and linens and diapers that efficient, decent good mommies lovingly prepare for their awaited angels. All items in the layette are, of course, hypoallergenic and thrice-washed in environmentally friendly detergent (bonus marks if by hand). They are in soothing, gender-neutral colours and preferably sewn from organic hemp or similar culturally appropriate and fairly traded materials.

Should Mommy know what gender her unborn child is before it is born (itself a sign of unworthiness: good mommies don't care about that), she would still not want to smother her offspring with outdated gender expectations, leaving yellow, green, and white as the only appropriate colour options.

Once your baby has been born and memories of restful sleep recede into your distant past, the romance of hand laundering the layette fades somewhat. Before you know it, Bad Mommy is throwing baby's clothes in—*gasp!*—the general laundry. Her next crime may well be to dress her boy in blue or daughter in pink.

As Bad Mommy bumbles further down the path of regressive clothing choices, she might even venture into the world of unnatural fibres. While seemingly practical and thrifty, Bad Mommy will never be sure that microscopic specks of artificial thread haven't inserted themselves under the skin of her hapless spawn, thereby setting them up for a lifetime of horrifying allergies.

Bad Mommy may choose to purchase brand-new clothing, so as to avoid the hidden parasites and general grodiness factor of second-hand duds. But in so doing, she damages the family karma by participating in the ugly reality of the sweatshop labour that produces most new clothing. Bad Mommy may have thought she was buying a nice T-shirt, but instead has corrupted her soul with vicarious child abuse. Furthermore, giving in to social urges for brand-name clothing helps trap Bad Mommy into an endless cycle of materialism that leads to financial strain and mindless consumerism.

Should Mommy choose to buy second-hand to avoid this karma trap, she will most likely cause grievous harm to her young by exposing them to the toxic laundry washing and disease-ridden effluvium of the previous child, whose death in the clothes likely lead the guilt-filled parents to donate all the clothing to the thrift shop.

Colleen, a forty-two-year-old mother of a nine-year-old boy and six-year-old girl, struggles with the issue of clothing her children. Financially, buying everyone a new and ever-changing wardrobe is simply not an option. Dressing her family is about "juggling priorities. The kids need to be dressed; my husband needs to be dressed." Colleen clothes her family through "sales racks, thrift stores, and discounts…the only new things they get are at deep discount at the end of the season." Colleen and her husband both make decent wages, but the funds are simply not there to pay retail. How do other families do it? "Maybe they can have grandparents to buy them that shit. Maybe they don't eat or drink booze, or put gas in their car."

Colleen has no compunction about clothing her children in second-hand clothes. She does insist that they are washed the instant they come home. "I rip off the labels and into the hot water they go." Colleen's children aren't even pre-teens yet, yet the pressure is starting to build. Although the boy doesn't care what he wears (also potentially problematic), her "daughter will find something totally inappropriate" (her preference runs to feathers) and demand to wear it. Colleen also has to veto the written word. "Messages on kids' shirts like 'sexy' and 'porn star'—that's gross. That's child abuse."

Forty-two-year-old Olivia is the mommy of a nine-year-old girl. Her child went through the usual phases of pretty dresses until she attended school. The first warning sign occurred when her then six-year-old daughter pulled her jeans far down over her hips. When Olivia protested, she was told, "It's fashion, Mommy," to which Olivia responded, "Pull them up; I don't care what fashion is." Olivia's daughter wanted high heels last year at age eight. Olivia doesn't have cable and they don't have fashion magazines, so she is not sure where this is coming from. Further to this, Olivia is really "hacked off at shops" and sales assistants who swoop down on her child, offering her this garment or that. "I don't like that...finding myself on the sidelines, trying to assert my authority. I'm the mediator of what she wears, not you."

Olivia's child is very interested in personal grooming and goes to great lengths to prepare for an outing. "I'm amazed at how long she spends in front of the mirror. It's quite odd." Olivia's child is learning how to push Mommy's buttons. If she sees something she wants, she will be direct: "I need that so badly. I want that sweater. It will make me so happy." Olivia says her daughter will compare herself to her peers: "She's got nothing to wear and her friends all have nicer clothing than her." Olivia also fears that this is just the beginning. "I've often quite fancied school uniforms," says this Bad Mommy.

Chapter 15

Bad Mommy Moves Her Baby

The animosity that women feel towards each other does not end with high school. The jealous need to one-up other women extends far into the mommy lifestyle. Instead of checking out new cars or new designer handbags, a mommy will soon find herself sucked into the world of strollers and other baby-moving vehicles. It's not enough to have a child and parent it well; the child must always be presented in the most flattering manner, like staging a home you intend to put on the market.

To the non-initiate or first-time parent, it seems seductively simple. You might (foolishly) assume that all babies travel in strollers until they can walk independently, at which point they are then carried on their parents' shoulders in a totem-pole-like fashion.

Nothing could be so simple. First, the choice of stroller (if a stroller is to be used at all) is paramount. What kind of bling does the stroller come with? Is it convertible? Does it have a leather, sheep-fur, zip-out liner? Can it go over rough terrain, or is it limited to a mall? Can it be opened with one hand while holding onto a wiggling baby with the other? If a mommy chooses a two-seater, will it be a side-by-side that cannot be manoeuvred through a space narrower than an airplane hanger? If it is a stacked tandem (one child over the other), what will this do to the hierarchical birth order of the children? If it is a "sit and stand" type with an older child clinging to the back while the toddler rides in front, will the older child unclip themselves and dart into oncoming traffic?

Some mommies refuse to use strollers. Putting your child in a stroller removes the child from your arms, heartbeat, and all-important personal body smells. Strollers are abusive in that they inhibit a healthy attachment to a primary caregiver. A stroller is also lower to the ground than the adults, subtly communicating to the child that they have low status and have to gaze upwards to face a dominant adult. A truly cherished and attached baby will only be carried skin-to-skin at adult eye level.

In response to this need to carry babies, a wide variety of slings and wraps have entered the marketplace along with the more traditional snuggly front packs. These slings look good and work well for a tiny baby, if you can actually figure out how to get them on (an impossible task similar to doing origami with a wet seal). "Wearing" your baby ensures that the mother-child bond is strengthened throughout the day, lessening the risk of psychopathic behaviour in later life.

Of course, slings only really work until your baby is about fifteen pounds or three months old. After this point, you will start to lose circulation in various parts of your body due to the constriction of major arteries by your large baby. Extended sling carrying of a heavy child can compress discs in the back, causing early osteoporosis or pinched nerves. As well, carried babies will have the expectation that they will be "carried" throughout life, leading to a pattern of dependent relationships and unhealthy self-soothing behaviours, all because of you, Bad Mommy.

Should you decide that the stroller is the only option, be prepared for an overwhelming and confusing new experience. Shopping for strollers is worse than shopping for cars. Mommies fall victim to stroller envy. The pressure to upgrade to the off-road, wireless stroller with the built-in cappuccino maker is enough to break the toughest mommy. Some strollers come equipped with a hermetically sealed plastic bubble so that the child is safe from smog and toxins and the mommy is safe from hearing the child; it's kind of a mobile win-win situation for the up-and-coming bad mommy.

Regardless of how you choose to move your baby, feel comforted in the knowledge that others will judge you and find your choices lacking.

Kitty, age twenty-seven, wanted a natural approach to raising her children. She attended an "attachment parenting" support group and was invited to join a discussion of strollers. Kitty was "made to feel horribly, horribly disgustingly guilty" over her use of a stroller with her child. According to the other mommies, she was "pushing her baby away from her" by using a stroller, both physically and, more important, symbolically. Mommies who use strollers were described as "disconnected" from their babies. If a mommy was not touching her baby at all times, how could she be expected to read its cues? The child might even have to—*gasp*—cry to get Mommy's attention.

Kitty was shocked when the conversation turned to the ultimate evil, the jogging stroller. Jogging strollers are so uncomfortable for baby. According to the mommies, selfish mommies who put their own slim aspirations over of their babies' comfort could almost be considered abusive.

Several months after this encounter, Kitty spied the woman heading the discussion in a crowded market with her own child in a stroller. Kitty was secretly delighted and attempted in vain to make eye contact with the bad mommy as she rushed away.

When Kathleen was expecting her child, a well-intentioned friend gave her a "sling" at her baby shower. The sling was the hip new way of carrying your child to encourage bonding and breastfeeding while walking. "Slings are great if you don't have breasts and your belly isn't hanging right out there," says Kathleen. "It's all about breast clearance." As a well-endowed, short woman, the space for a baby and a sling and two massive boobies simply did not exist. Her son was "never fetal" and was a very long, splayed-out child: "He's long; I'm short. Trying to bend him into the right shape was impossible!" To make matters worse, the sling did work for her husband, who has no boobs. "Fuck him!"

Obnoxiously, Daddy happily carried the child in the sling for ten months, attracting all type of females in the park after some über-mommy showed him the secrets of sling use at the beach. As for the bonding and breastfeeding that is supposed to happen in a sling? "There was no bonding," admits Kathleen, "and when people tell you to breastfeed in a sling, I want you to know that you can't if you are sporting an E-cup. If you have to dig past the kid to dig out your tit, it's just not going to work."

Chapter 16

Bad Car Seat Mommy

Do you remember the joy of riding in cars when you were a child? Sitting in the front seat on your mommy's lap, her arms firmly wrapped around your waist as a "seat belt"? Racing for the coveted wheel-well seat that would prop you up for a better view during that ride down the freeway in the back of an open pickup truck? Ah, the good old days when bad mommies ruled with an iron fist!

The old saying "ignorance is bliss" could not be more appropriate than when one is considering the car seat. The intricacies of car seat rules are a tangled and ever-changing web that will drive any sane person insane, let alone a bad mommy!

Children need to ride in cars with their mommies, that much is clear. Children should not sit in the front seat if there are air bags on the passenger side that cannot be turned off. This too is clear to most (everyone nod). Of course, this may be a challenge if your only vehicle is a pickup truck or a two-seater car or a sports car of any type. However, should you be foolish enough to own one of these, you will quickly learn that none of these vehicles are conducive to the mommy lifestyle anyway.

The only place a child can sit in a car without tempting immediate death is the back seat, in a properly fitting child-restraint system. If a child is not properly harnessed in a properly functioning and fitting car seat, should anything go wrong (which it will undoubtedly), Bad Mommy's child will suffer permanent injuries, and perhaps even death, all because of her extreme negligence and ignorance.

Infants need to be placed in a rear-facing bucket or convertible car seat. Little babies will lack the neck strength to keep their necks straight, which will cause their heads to loll alarmingly forward. However, do not be tricked into purchasing those cute little neck positioning head condoms you can buy to address this problem, as they will actually interfere with the correct positioning of the car seat and will irreparably harm your child.

A long, long time ago in another era (five years ago), the common wisdom suggested keeping children rear-facing in their car seats until they were six months old. This rule, of course, has now changed, and children apparently need to be kept rear-facing until they are one year old. Do not fret about memorizing these numbers! By the time you read this, children will likely wait until after their sixteenth birthdays to become forward-facing.

The whole obsession and joy of turning a baby

to face forward is that they suddenly become happy—for the most part—and stop screaming so much when they are turned around. While a baby is rear-facing, they will most likely screech a great deal. This can be mildly distracting for a good mommy who may try to entertain her squalling car-infant with a variety of mirrors, stimulating black-and-white faces and patterns, and Lamaze toys that dance in a stimulating eccentric rhythm in the back of the vehicle. However, this good mommy has been short-sighted. In a car accident, these stimulating playthings will become projectiles that will pierce the child's body or decapitate the child and/or driver.

Once Bad Mommy's child has hit the magic size, whatever that may be (don't worry, it will still be wrong and woefully inadequate whatever it is), children and their car seats are flipped forward-facing and the child joins the world of vehicular stimulation. Everyone is now happy, but are they really safe? If the car seat was not purchased new, how does Bad Mommy know if it was ever in an accident? If her car seat was in an accident, the warranty is now void and the seat is probably useless. Really, why do you think someone was trying to get rid of it? Even if it hasn't been in an accident, is Bad Mommy certain it has not been recalled? The recall list on car seats is frightening. What kind of mommy checks these regularly? (Not a bad one, that's for sure.)

Should Mommy have dodged both of these

car-seat bullets and her car seat is in pristine shape and is not recalled, how does she truly know if her child is correctly buckled into the seat? The art of the "car-seat buckle" is a rarely discussed, yet arcane skill. If the child has too many or too few clothing items on, the buckle will not nestle the approved "two-finger width" from the child's abdomen. Any mishap in the car and the child will submarine, a charming term here used to describe the action in which a child's body is forced under the car seat restraints due to faulty positioning (and a bad mommy) and is squeezed out the other side of the car seat in a toothpaste-like fashion.

Should Mommy actually learn how to reach the coveted two-finger width with no problem, never fear! Her child can still be at risk because of her nascent disregard. In the US, car seats do not have to have a "tether strap," an optional strap attaching the back of the car seat to a bolt in the back of the car. Although mandatory in Canada, many cars made outside of Canada do not include the proper hardware for installing tether straps. If Bad Mommy has not installed the tether strap or, heaven forbid purchased a vehicle without the proper bolting latch system, her child and their car seat will likely be ejected from her vehicle at the next red light.

Do not think that Mommy is out of the woods once her child outgrows the car seat. Children then move into the mysterious and often-misunderstood world of the booster seat. In many areas, booster seats are not mandatory but are suggested for safety. That kind of mixed message just adds to this car-seat confusion. Should Bad Mommy purchase a booster seat that has not been recalled or in a car accident, it will likely not fit her child correctly. Children are crafty and do not like the adult seat belts used with their booster seats, since they cut into their necks. Most children cleverly avert this problem by tucking the offending shoulder belt behind their back, where the entire system is now rendered useless (yet comfortable). Of course, if Bad Mommy just puts her booster-sized child in a car with no booster seat, the adult seat belt will simply decapitate them in any type of accident.

Never fear, soon your child will be old enough to join you in the front seat of the car (at 100 pounds) where the air bag will deploy and take you both out. The jury is still out on airbags anyway, so you know what that means! At least you won't have to worry about anything then, Bad Mommy.

Thirty-eight-year-old Sunshine didn't know that car seats had expiration dates. "What are they, yoghurt?" A spendthrift in all ways, Sunshine's deep love for thrift extended to her children and their never-ending need for accoutrement. Recently, when attempting to donate her son's booster seat—procured many years earlier at a garage sale—to the Salvation Army, she was stopped in her tracks by the man at the loading door. "We can't take THAT," he said with derision. "Those have been illegal for years!" Sunshine was deeply chagrined and went online to look into this matter further. "Apparently, there's a whole nest of rules and regulations with car seats. It's way beyond airbags and boosters. Thank God I never knew and my kids are big enough now!"

Recently, Sunshine had to drive her six-year-old nephew to the airport. He came without a car seat, and Sunshine had already turfed her illegal and apparently neglectful booster seat. "What was I supposed to do?" This Bad Mommy is glad that her children don't need car seats anymore: "It's a wonder I never killed them."

Olivia, the mother of a nine-year-old girl, initially "worried a lot" about her child's car seat and car seats in general. However, neither she nor anyone she knew actually seemed to understand the mystery of the car seat. Most often, Olivia would click her child in and think, "Oh fuck, I hope that's all right!" Olivia admits to car-seat hypocrisy. She would fiercely debate detailed car-seat facts with her friends but in reality had no idea. She didn't even own a scale and so had no idea what her child weighed.

Olivia says, "My biggest concern was how dirty it was." Her husband would "go off" on her about letting their child eat in the car (like a mommy has an option!) and the car seat was consequently absolutely filthy and smelled terrible.

This mommy describes experiencing "car-seat dilemma" in which a mommy has two children, her own and a friends', and one car seat. "It's a moral dilemma: who gets the car seat?" Organizing a play date with another child in a car seat is virtually impossible. Olivia is happy the car seat days are behind her, "the swapping car seats around...the nightmare of it all."

Chapter 17

Bad Vaccinating Mommy

Vaccination choices, if well researched, can provide a Bad Mommy with decades of guilt, anxiety, and second-guessing. Contrary to common belief, choosing to vaccinate is a very difficult decision if a mommy actually stops to think about it. The goalposts keep moving every year or so to guarantee that no choice she makes in terms of vaccination will be good enough. Ever.

Vaccines are little bits of poison suspended in dubious—sometimes even more poisonous—liquids that are injected into your baby's skin to prevent sickness. The problem is, children can get sicker from the vaccine itself than they would have from the sickness that they never got. For example, we can consider the chicken pox vaccine and its nemesis, the chicken pox. A typical child with the pox will be slightly miserable for about four days, spotty and itchy for a couple of more days, then fine. However, a child with a bad chicken pox vaccine reaction can, in a worst case scenario, get really, really sick and die, so what is a mommy to do?

If you bite the bullet and vaccinate, there is also some question as to whether or not vaccinations will work in a couple of years. Just as your child reaches adolescence and starts really mingling with others, the protective factors of childhood vaccines may wear off, thus exposing your germ-free child to a host of pathogens for which his body was never given the opportunity to gain natural immunity, Bad Mommy.

Children can get really sick from the other stuff in the vaccine too. How many bad mommies know that many vaccines still contain mercury (known as thiomersal) as a preservative, which many believe can potentially cause autism or other horrible neurological diseases in children? The connection between autism and mercury has not been settled, but there are active class-action lawsuits from parents of children with autism against the producers of the MMR (measles, mumps, and rubella) vaccine, which is usually administered to children who are around eighteen months of age. Coincidentally—or not—this is the age at which symptoms of autism start to appear. Sure, the medical community is denying the connection, but they deny lots of stuff that ends up being true.

The risk could be minimal, but do you feel like testing it out on your kids, Bad Mommy?

Autism isn't the only concern of parents who vaccinate. Some children actually die from adverse reactions to vaccination. Shockingly, injecting a pathogen into the body of an infant may harm the child! Every year, several children do die as a result of "adverse" vaccination reactions.

Even if the vaccine does not kill or damage your child for life, many folks question how long they will last (if at all). Lots of children get chicken pox after they have had the vaccine. Measles outbreaks abound in children who were immunized as babies. Periodically, there will be an outbreak of something routinely vaccinated against, such as whooping cough. The first fingers will point to the bad mommies who have not vaccinated against these illnesses for selfish fear of death or injury to their young. However, it usually turns out that the vector of infection were children who had been immunized in the first place, but for some mysterious reason the immunization did not "take." These bad mommies not only subjected their children to the injection of potentially life-threatening poison, but the actual vaccine did not even work!

Some mommies, paralyzed by fear of vaccine damage, will not vaccinate at all! These bad mommies are playing inoculation roulette. Yes, there is a good chance that their unvaccinated children will never run into one of these nasty childhood diseases at some point in time. Of course, there is also an excellent chance that they will, in fact, run into such a disease. Should this occur, the very diagnosis will expose Mommy for the bad mommy she is.

Mommies have been charged with medical neglect for not vaccinating their child on schedule. Children have been removed from their mommies' care because of the choice to not vaccinate. This is serious stuff!

If you vaccinate your child, you are potentially dooming them to lifelong neurological impairment, mental health problems, or death. If you do not vaccinate your children, you are potentially dooming them to lifelong neurological impairment, mental health problems, or death. Your only option is to move to a biosphere somewhere and lock them up until they can emerge as adults.

Colleen, a forty-two-year-old mother of a nine-year-old son and a six-year-old daughter, has a harrowing tale of vaccination. When her son was twenty-four months old, he had a strong reaction to his pertussis (whooping cough) vaccination that included a spiked fever and a seizure. Her son has been closely monitored and continues to have a seizure disorder and subsequent neuro-developmental issues. Initially, Colleen did not suspect the vaccine might be the culprit until her doctor expressed some hesitancy in vaccinating her child again. "No one has ever said it was the vaccine, but no one has said it was not." Colleen has subsequently made the decision to not vaccinate this child again or his little sister at all.

Now Colleen feels that her family has been "red flagged" as some kind of non-vaccinating freaks. "The health nurses have phoned, saying, 'Your kid is not up to date.' I tell them that I am well aware and that I am making an informed decision." They think Colleen is being a bad mommy by "neglecting" to vaccinate, but she feels that vaccinating would be negligent and potentially life threatening. People have insinuated that she is putting her children at risk by not vaccinating; family members have asked, "What if she dies? Won't you feel bad if she dies?" To this, Colleen replies, "Really."

Scarlett, a thirty-six-year-old mother of two, has suffered over the question of vaccination with her children. Before children, she thought, "Of course I was going to vaccinate; it never occurred to me that there was a choice." It was her midwife during her first pregnancy who planted the initial "seeds of vaccination doubt" in her mind. Confused by the mixed messages about vaccinations, Scarlett and her husband eventually decided to "selectively vaccinate," meaning they vaccinate for some diseases, but not others. "I spent the first two years being tortured about it," Scarlett explains. "There is huge societal pressure to vaccinate but very good evidence to show that vaccinations can cause problems. I felt really torn." Scarlett's heard it all, including the de rigueur "How are you going to feel when your baby dies of whooping cough?" from her own mommy. Thanks!

No matter what vaccination choice Scarlett made, someone wasn't happy. "All those granola-eating bark-wearing hippie mommies were horrified that I was considering some vaccinations, and my normal working friends were also horrified I wasn't vaccinating on schedule!" Scarlett admits that she "still worries about it." Every year at school, she has to fill out forms admitting her vaccination neglect. Scarlett says, "I'm beyond guilt; it's moved into confusion and worry."

Chapter 18

Bad Dental Care Mommy

Have you ever tried to bathe a cat? Brushing a young child's teeth is roughly as pleasurable and effective. Good mommies know that from the moment of birth they are to use a fingertip lightly wrapped in gauze to wipe over baby's gums after every feeding. As the first precious tooth buds erupt, Good Mommy will gently and lovingly wipe each tooth from both sides with a fluoride-free organic cleanser. Baby will be put to bed with clean teeth and will not be fed through the night to prevent the dreaded "night nursing" syndrome, a hallmark of the bad mommy, in which the infant's teeth slowly turn into dental mush after months of gently marinating in nighttime booby milk.

The truth is, unless you are a professional dental-care technician, your children's teeth are probably not up to snuff. Who in their right mind would wake up a sleeping baby who has finally passed out after screaming for three hours to "gently swab out the mouth"? Not this bad mommy! Further to this, what kind of mommy would refuse a hungry baby in the middle of the night? We all know nighttime munchies are the worst!

Bad mommies tend to adopt a "just say yes if it will get me back to sleep" policy. Nighttime nursing is not encouraged by dental professionals, as the milk has all night to pool on the teeth, causing untold damage. But really, they lose those teeth anyway, so who cares?

All of you bottle-using mommies can stop feeling smug right now. First, you are bad, since you are not breastfeeding (please see Bad Mommy and Her Boobies). Second, you and your evil plastic nipples are also the cause of dental damage. Putting anything but water in a bottle will cause "bottle mouth," a charming syndrome where the front teeth will rot in a parabolic arc roughly the same shape as a baby bottle.

Some bad mommies use a "bottle propping" technique to get the most out of their day. By propping a baby up with a tasty sweet bottle of juice (bonus marks for pop), Mommy can nicely get through her day and baby can get to work at exploring the world of being toothless, once again.

Even if you have lovingly cared for your baby's teeth since eruption, you are still in for some dental treats. If you ever needed to take penicillin during your pregnancy (Bad Mommy!), your baby may end up with stained and uneven enamel. Antibiotics given to pregnant or nursing bad mommies can also stain your darling's nascent teeth, although no one will mention it to you at the time.

Do not think you will escape dental damnation by using fluoride. The jury is out on whether or not it is helpful or some sort of evil poison. By the time it is much too late to make a difference, we will find out definitively if all these years of fluoride treatment have caused permanent, lifelong damage to the developing bodies and brains of our children or simply toughened up the enamel as promised.

Once the teeth actually make it out unrotten and undamaged (like that is going to happen), you'll be paying the price for weaning them too early or too late or not at all when your child's unmet oral fixation leads to thumb-sucking or blanket-licking. These nasty habits might mean that your child will need orthodontia.

Headgear and unwieldy braces make brushing a newborn's gums seem like a walk in the park. Eating popcorn will never be the same! Let's not forget the cost associated with orthodontia. Your child can either have a college education or straight teeth. By the time you cajole and massage them out of orthodontia, they will then start ruining their teeth with adult vices such as coffee, and the cycle of dental damage will begin once again.

Lilah, aged thirty-seven, is a mother of a two-year-old boy and says, "Kids come without teeth, so it's an emergent issue." Lilah was a well-intentioned mommy who honestly did her best for her son's teeth (or so she thought). Reading about the dangers of exposing a child to fluoride, she would instead let him play with an organic tooth "polish" made of boiled-down pectin and apple sauce. It turns out that boiled-down pectin isn't as wholesome as one might think. "I was trying, but I was failing."

Lilah's file was flagged by the public health nurse as a potential "problem mommy" when it was discovered she was—*gasp*—breastfeeding her one-year-old. The nurse and local dentist staged a "fluoride intervention" and showed Lilah a graphic video of babies with rotting teeth. She was told sternly, "Your son is at severe risk for dental issues...hopefully, it's not too late." Lilah was told that tooth decay is the number one reason for children under the age of five to go under general anesthetic. After three months of diligent brushing, Lilah went back to the dentist to show her progress. They were impressed but now insist she start to floss her baby's teeth. "Why don't I just floss my cat's teeth instead?" says this Bad Mommy.

Bad Dental Mommy of children aged fourteen and eleven, thirty-eight-year-old Sunshine states, "I have failed on so many levels." To the typical dental lecture about only feeding babies water at night, she replies, "How are you supposed to do that when you are lying naked in bed with your boob hanging out?" The first time she took her daughter to the dentist, it was cavities, cavities, cavities. She was told in no uncertain terms that "breastfeeding at night was BAD, and I needed to wean my daughter." This confused Sunshine, who had heard from other non-dental sources that breastfeeding was, in fact, good.

Sunshine's dentist interrogated her further as her children aged and their teeth crumbled—was she letting them eat fruit leather and raisins? This neglectful mommy, thinking that fruit leather and raisins were "natural" choices, had allowed her tots access to these substances. Tsk, tsk. Bad Mommies, as all dentists and Good Mommies know, who give fruit leather and raisins along with nighttime nursing are bordering on dental neglect.

Sunshine's dentist, so horrified by the number of cavities in her children's teeth, has proposed that her family is likely a carrier for some nasty dental bacteria that is passed along from mother to baby. The infected mommy's mouth was probably infesting the baby with nasty flora. Of course, that would be Sunshine's fault, but it actually makes some sort of horrible intuitive sense if she thinks about her own mother's bad teeth as well as her own. According to her dentist, the practice of taking a bite of food and then giving it to your child actually infects the child—forever—with this bacteria and also starts a charming rotten-toothed family tradition.

Sunshine is worried that her youngest child needs braces, as his teeth appear to point in different directions. She hasn't gone down that path yet but is concerned that braces are a "big hairy deal." They come with many time-consuming and impossible food instructions including ludicrous notions such as "apples needing to be cut and peeled." Her dentist has had a preliminary chat with her about the "braces lifestyle" and presented Sunshine (in a slightly threatening way) with a large and grim colour photo of a child's rotting, braces-filled mouth—clearly someone's Bad Mommy did not make them floss correctly. The dentist lectured her on the importance of flossing. Since getting kids to floss regular teeth is such a walk in the park, she is sure getting her son to floss teeth with braces will "be so much fun for us all!" Besides being aesthetically pleasing, braces are also outrageously expensive: Phase One was $4,000, and that's only for the upper teeth.

Chapter 19

Bad Mommy at Work, Bad Mommy at Play

Working outside of the home while you have children is arguably one of the most challenging elements of parenting. Both parents (assuming there are two of you) cannot work full-time outside of the home without something big blowing up and quickly (hopefully not the children).

Unfortunately, because of the financial realities of our world, most mommies will have to go "back to work" (like you ever actually stopped working when you went on "leave" to have your child). When this happens, you will know the true meaning of being a bad mommy. Working mothers have no time. Period. Multi-tasking is absolutely necessary but leaves no room for mistakes. A working mommy can send a fax, type an email, check in with her children on her cellphone, and order tonight's dinner simultaneously. Alas, by doing all of these at the same time, there will be serious quality control issues. You can have it all, but not all at once.

Quality child care is the true bane of any mommy's life. The guilt and anxiety of leaving your precious children in the hands of strangers to, at best, get lice, chicken pox, impetigo, and poor social skills and, at worst, be molested or become part of a satanic child-murdering ring is enough to send many women back to the home, where an equally unpleasant fate awaits them: the fate of the stay-at-home mommy.

Child care for a baby can easily cost $1,000 per month (if you are extremely lucky), and child care for an older child can be $700 per month. You can see why staying at home starts to make a lot of sense to many mommies. Even before-and after-school care for a school-aged child is about $400 per month. Multiply that by two or three and there is not much room to move financially. We work to pay someone else for the privilege of neglecting and abusing our children, which should be our own prerogative. It's ludicrous!

Working mommies consider stay-at-home mommies "the enemy." Stay-at-Home Mommy and child with their darling Mommy-Child matching outfits, their circle time at the library, and their outings to the aquarium with healthy hand-packed picnics of organic tidbits make working bad mommies seethe with feelings of inadequacy and worthlessness.

The stay-at-home mommy's lot is no better though. She has traded her identity, career, and life aspirations for play groups and storytime. Suddenly, her PhD is worthless; she's just another bland face at circle time. Work friends stop calling. Soon enough, they won't even recognize her on the street, as she completes her metamorphosis into a house Frau by adopting the mommy uniform of jeans and a T-shirt.

No more trips to the hairdresser for Stay-at-Home Mommy; her roots grow out and, as her transformation completes itself, she may adopt the ponytail and baseball cap look favoured by her kind to hide the grease and grey in her hair.

Stay-at-Home Mommy has no friends outside of the mommies of her children's play dates. She quickly loses her place in the workplace, and if she ever chooses to return, she will be outdated and un-hirable. By saving her child from Satanists and child abusers, she will give up everything else that ever mattered to her. She will see her arch-nemesis, the working bad mommy with her nice, dry-cleaned clothes and updated highlights, dropping her smiling child off at daycare with a jaunty backwards wave, and she will seethe with feelings of inadequacy and worthlessness. She will then turn to drink or other forms of self-medication and will continue her own personal journey into becoming a bad mommy too.

Of course, no one ever suggests that Daddy stay home with the children and Mommy go back to work. Despite all the lip service we pay to women's rights and equality, when the chips are down, the men bolt back to their quiet haven of work as quickly as possible. For all their faults, they certainly aren't fools! They seem immune to the pangs of guilt and anxiety that plague working mommies. Should you have one of those rare species of man who actually wants to stay home with the children, never fear! You are clearly a bad mommy too! Bad Working Mommy with Stay-at-Home Daddy is obviously totally worthless as a woman, mother, and human being. When this bad mommy comes home from the office to a clean house, happy children, and a good househusband, she will know that she has officially become redundant. This mommy is not only bad, she is completely useless and easily replaced by, of all things, a man.

Furthermore, daddies who stay home with children get extra bonus points for "babysitting." Why is it babysitting when it is his own children? The universe is full of such unanswerable mysteries! Nothing is quite as magnetic and sexy as a man at a park with a baby. Your stay-at-home daddy will become the life of the playground, a complete chick magnet with a busy round of "coffee dates" with the other cool mommies who wouldn't even give you the time of day.

Some mommies are in the "enviable" position of having grandparents provide child care while they go to work. Many women foolishly resent these women for their free family child care. Do not be irrational and fall into this trap. Remember that there is no such thing as "free child care." If it is her in-laws providing this "free" service, they are most likely secretly undermining her place and status in the family in a covert, underhanded plan to take the children as their own and eventually rid themselves of Bad Mommy. If it is her own parents providing this "service," they are likely replaying the same bad patterns of behaviour they first exhibited with the previous generation (and didn't get right). How happy was your own childhood? Going to let them have another go at the new generation?

Clara, a forty-one-year-old mother of two, now works from home after years of working in an office. Many people seem mystified by this decision. "When people find out I'm working at home and my kids are in daycare they think I am a bad mommy." People have bluntly asked, "Did you really want your children or did you want your career?" Clara states, "I've had it from both sides." The other working mommies think that she is a slacker who can help them with after-school care, since she is only "working from home," and the stay-at-home mommies don't understand why she can't do coffee and play dates.

Clara made the switch to a home office when her eldest was two years old. Her employer saw her as "a mommy and not an employee." She says, "It's a battle for the working mommy. I can't work overtime, and employers do not want to hear that—they question your priorities. Why should they hire a mommy?" Quitting her job and reconfiguring her work has not been without substantial cost. Clara admits: "I'm not making as much money now. I had to take a huge pay cut—at least half my salary—to work from home."

Although being a working mommy has its challenges, Clara would never be a stay-at-home mommy. "They are batty. They are nutcases. They can't carry on a conversation beyond, 'Do you want some juicey?'" The brief time spent with stay-at-homes was frightening to her. She says, "They are not even pulled together: look how they dress...! Stay-at-home moms have not thought critically about the world. How long has it been since they have read a book or—*gasp*—the newspaper? I couldn't take the pressure; I didn't want to be one of those people."

When thirty-six-year-old Scarlett was nearing the end of her first pregnancy, she requested a few extra (unpaid) weeks off from her boss. Prior to this, she had been employee of the month. The response? "If we do it for you, we will have to do it for all the women." Thus began Scarlett's journey as a working mommy.

Finances dictated an early return to work for Scarlett and resulted in huge guilt: "It's hard leaving your little people behind." This was a difficult decision and not a popular one. "Lots of my friends were deciding to stay home. They had the privilege of making that choice, and I had to go back." Going back to work was not an easy choice either. "It's pretty stark, working full-time and travelling with business; this year, I'm missing Halloween."

Scarlett reports having many run-ins with "smug stay-at-home moms" at her school who gently chide her for missing a PAC meeting, or being late for buying tickets for a school event. Scarlett brushes aside their smug attitude: "If I wasn't working so much, I would have proper priorities...I guess that's what they think."

Scarlett feels for the stay-at-homes. "Their children are now about ten, and they are trying to get back into the workforce, but they realize there is no place for them there. They are jealous of me...of my polish. I get to dress up and interact with adults. But I'm jealous of them: they get to sit in the classroom and cut out pictures." Scarlett feels bad for her former antagonists. "So many stay-at-homes are so frumpy. What happens to them? They become invisible."

Chapter 20

Bad Mommy and Money

For the most part, we live paycheque to paycheque, just like our mommies did. "Why do we live just like Mommy?" you might ask. The answer is simple. You grow up to have just about the same socio-economic status as your parents unless you really screw up (of course, totally possible, in fact, likely) or are really lucky (much more doubtful).

This means that our children will grow up to have the same socio-economic status that we now currently "enjoy." You know, all that disposable income, all the trips abroad, the fancy private schools, personal horseback lessons, and British au pairs.

The truth is that most mommies and their families are struggling to keep their heads above water. Making it to the next paycheque without going into overdraft or abusing your Visa is an increasingly rare event. We "borrow" from our mortgages and extend and blend the amount of credit that we take on just to make ends meet. The notion of a savings account or a rainy-day fund seems old-fashioned and kind of cute.

Children are a very expensive little habit. Good mommies know this and invest in an education savings fund for their children from birth, hoping to defray some of the financial burden in the long term. When the children of these good mommies finish high school, there will be a nice fat fund waiting to support them through university. These pampered youngsters can relax and enjoy their stress-free years of university. However, these good mommies don't get off scot-free! By financially providing for these children, these mommies are teaching their young that handouts are everywhere, and they will, thus, never appreciate the value of money as adults.

Bad Mommy does not invest in her children's educational future. There is no extra money, so the actual thought of putting money away for the future seems insane. By not investing early in her child's financial future, Bad Mommy will force her young to either abandon dreams of higher education (cursing future generations to a lifetime of lower socio-economic status) or her children will have no choice but to get scholarships to pay their own way in school. The only way they can do this, of course, is to have no social lives or hobbies outside of studying, which will have the effect of turning them into obese loners who will thus have no friends, social skills, or interests.

Should you be one of those lucky mommies who has a lot of money, your children will suffer terribly too. You will correctly fear that people will only want to befriend them because of perceived benefits of befriending money, and they will never have true and genuine relationships. By relying on nannies and tutors, Bad Money Mommy's child will come to expect a legion of paid helpers to be at their beck and call and will develop an attitude of entitlement that will keep them toasty warm in their isolated adult lives.

As teenagers, the children of Bad Money Mommy will likely be kidnapped and held for ransom by desperate gang members who know they are rich kids. If Bad Money Mommy gets them back alive, they will never trust another person again and will turn to drugs and self-abuse for company, or better yet, develop Stockholm Syndrome and now identify with the kidnappers, turning on their bad mommy for the years of financial abuse they suffered at her hands.

Do not think you poor mommies are getting off lightly either! Yes, your children will understand what it means to work for their money, which is a good thing...because working for their money is something they are going to have to do for the rest of their long and weary, joyless lives. Because of the poor neighbourhood they are raised in and public schools they attend, they will develop a peer group of riff-raff and future gang members. Everyone knows that parents lose most of their influence by the time their child is twelve. Your once-loving child will go from being in your arms to being jumped into some gang and either turned out to work the streets or converted into an urban soldier in some sort of petty turf war, Bad Mommy!

Regardless of whether you are rich or poor, by living in North America, you are, by definition, rich. Compared to third-world living conditions, the poorest family here is ridiculously wealthy. As most of us do not share what we have with the third world, regardless of our wealth level, we are adding to the financial inequality in this world and making our environmental footprint on this earth larger than it has to be. Our children's karma is suffering simply by living in a developed country. The only way to deal with this inequality is for your whole family to move to the third world to do volunteer work for a prolonged period. Of course, Mommy and her children will then likely contract some horrible virus or worm that enters through the feet while wading in shallow water, come home with a clear karma, and die three days later in their beds. You just can't win.

Star, a thirty-four-year-old mother of an eleven-year-old daughter, feels "despair" when she considers the socio-economic situation in which she is currently embroiled. Star works full-time, and her husband has been unemployed for several years. They live in a trailer with an addition; it is "very shameful" for Star: "I have huge house shame." They drive a 1990 Ford Tempo. "I have car shame too," explains Star.

Star's daughter is becoming more and more aware of the disparities between her family's financial situation and that of her peers. It doesn't help that she has "rich friends" whose parents are able to provide for their every whim. Star's daughter is now asking for big-ticket items. "She wants the eighty-dollar jeans and the one-hundred-and-fifty-dollar shoes, her own cellphone, DVD player, electric scooter...." For her next birthday, her daughter wants a "skating party and a movie and friends overnight and presents."

Star is not sure where the money is going to come from. She has a couple of friends who "re-mortgage every four years so that they can buy things for their kids." Star is resentful that these mommies have done this, setting the bar impossibly high. "I'm on a budget; this causes me lots of mommy guilt." Yesterday, she asked if I was saving for her university. I say, sure, but I'm not. How can I?"

Sara, a forty-one-year-old single mother of a ten-year-old girl, is personally living the financial roller coaster of parenting a child. Sara's daughter attends a school where most of her peers come from affluent families, unlike Sara, a single working mommy. "At times, it's been crippling; there is never enough, and you're it." It's not just the obvious costs that are bringing her down, it's the hidden costs such as birthday parties. Sara estimates she spent $2,000 last year alone on birthday gifts for children: the older her child gets, the more parties she is invited to. "I don't like to give icky presents. I've fallen into a trap," admits Sara.

Extracurricular activities are also outrageously expensive. Sara's daughter attends swimming lessons, which cost Sara $800 per year for the privilege of a heated pool and somewhat smaller classes. Most of the families in Sara's social group at the school have two parents: Mommy stays home (most likely doing bad things) and Daddy works and brings home the money. Sara's friends simply can't conceptualize the financial restraints that she faces on a day-to-day basis just to try and keep up with them.

Chapter 21

Bad Mommy and Culture

As everyone knows, speaking a single language forever limits your child's mind and vocational opportunities. The children of Europe are fortunate to dwell in that dialect-rich continent, with even the most unfortunate urchin speaking roughly five languages. If your child does not learn at least one secondary language before age ten, when the language centres in their brains fasten up, they will be doomed to unilingualism. Good mommies know that this is simply not acceptable. They will do whatever it takes to ensure that their children have a rich linguistic and cultural background by the time they reach kindergarten.

The only truly acceptable way for a child to learn a second language is in the home. A rich bilingual environment where both parents speak at least two languages in the home is the preferred situation. Good Mommy and her multilingual partner will banter across the dinner table in various languages, happily switching between them, and enjoying the subtle puns and inferences to be made from the witty repartee while their darling children watch in rapt ecstasy. If Good Mommy is not able to provide this optimal environment, her second choice would be full language immersion, preferably starting in pre-school, with a language tutor. Good Mommy will study her child's second language, making a game of naming various foods and objects around the home in this new tongue.

Some bad mommies think they can get away with late immersion by keeping their young away from a second language until they are in Grade Six or later! These poor youngsters will forever lag behind their truly bilingual comrades. As adults, important government posts will be denied to them because of their clumsy syntax and inability to grasp the finer nuances of the language that are only learned as a young child.

Should you be a truly bad mommy and only expose your child to a second language through the normal vectors of the school system, you will curse your child to an adult life of menial labour. They will never see their career advance beyond basic drudgery because of their pathetic lack of a second language.

By denying your child an infancy soaked in a minimum of two tongues, you will impoverish your child's life in a permanent way. Their brains, damaged by the lack of proper linguistic stimulation, will forever atrophy.

Providing cultural richness to your children extends beyond simple language acquisition. Children need to be exposed to cultural diversity in order to find their true path to happiness and fulfillment in their lives. A good mommy will take her child to all cultural events in her neighbourhood (bonus marks for having to travel!) and will ensure that the rich cultural heritage of their local melting pot of nations will be fully translated into a meaningful personal context for their child. A good mommy knows that every day is an opportunity for her to enrich her child's understanding of the world around her. Bad Mommy hopes that by leaving the TV on the Discovery Channel, her children might pick up some pointers about foreigners and their odd ways.

Annie, a thirty-six-year-old mother of an eight-year-old girl, lives in a biracial family. She is a typical WASP Canadian: "I'm a mishmash. I don't have a strong culture. There's no real food or dance associated with my roots." However, her husband is Korean, and his family "really pushes the Korean." Annie admits, "It should make me happy, but it really pisses me off. She [their daughter] identifies more with that culture. They push it on her; they think it is so much better. They make her feel that she and they are superior because of their culture." Annie's own heritage and culture are bowled over by this focus on all things Korean.

Because of the importance of cultural diversity to this family, Annie and her husband decided to enroll their child in a French school for kindergarten. Although she loved the idea of her child learning another language, communication with this school was more of a problem for the adults than the children. Annie ended up missing her child's Christmas concert because of an oversight on the school's part, so Annie and her husband pulled their daughter out of the program and moved her to a local school. "That makes me feel bad. She could have had this great chance to speak fluent French, but we pulled her."

Annie wants her child to also learn Korean, since her husband speaks the language and there is a Korean language school in the area. However, her husband will not get around to finding out about it. "He's lazy. It's our ultimate failure: we are lazy."

Pascal, a thirty-eight-year-old mother of two, has a "constant gnawing anxiety" about her children's lack of a second language, specifically French. Pascal was born in Quebec and was raised bilingual by her French-speaking mother. Her family was "proud Quebecois, and pro-separatist." Much to Pascal's extended family's horror, she is raising her children in an English-speaking home, culture, and school. The minute anyone learns Pascal is bilingual, they immediately assume that her children study French (as this is clearly the choice a good bilingual mommy would make). Pascal refuses to enroll her children in French immersion. The other parents who typically enroll their children in immersion are an elitist "French club," who get their "noses out of joint that we don't speak French at home."

The common sentiment is that Pascal is denying her kids the rich experience of being French. Her mother will ask her, "Why don't you talk to them in French?" The real answer: "I'm fucking lazy and I don't want to. It's too much work. I have to do the house and the kids and homework. If I have to start translating too, it will be too much. Let's jut admit it: I am lazy."

Although Pascal feels niggling guilt about her children's lack of rich cultural heritage, she is conflicted. "I'm selfish. I want to be the *je ne sais quoi* sexy French wife, but I don't want to work for it." Ultimately, Pascal admits, in terms of culture, "I do nothing. We celebrate the West Coast culture. When it rains, we stay inside; when it's nice, we go outdoors."

Chapter 22

Bad Mommy and TV

Before having children, we looked judgmentally upon bad mommies who allowed their children to watch TV. If and when you had children, you told yourself the evil TV would be barred from the home. Your child would only be read to and would listen to classical music from birth (maybe even before). Your home environment would be so stimulating and enriched that the entire notion of television would be foreign.

This resolve is passing, and it should be given the same credence as your January first promise to exercise more and eat well. Bad mommies quickly recognize the importance of TV (known in at least one home as cathode therapy) with the birth of their first child.

The TV and remote control are a mommy's new best friends and single-handedly help her get through those first stimulating months of breastfeeding and related small-animal-husbandry-like infant-related tedium. The real reason for the existence of daytime talk shows becomes abundantly clear when you are chained to a rocking chair by your boobies and a baby.

As her little one gets a little older, Mommy starts to realize the potential distraction power of this magnificent invention. Catering to the well-intentioned, you can easily buy *Baby Einstein* or *Baby Mozart* DVDs for your infant. By having your child watch these educational DVDs, you are actually stimulating their cerebral cortex: you are being a good mommy! As you enjoy the precious, free minutes of time to be snagged as your six-month-old sits propped up in their excersaucer, watching *Baby Einstein* instead of you (only you, just you), you start your journey on the slippery slope of cathode therapy and TV addiction.

As your child gets older, a whole new world of entertainment opens up to them. Most of these shows are—um—educational! By allowing Bobby to watch *Dora the Explorer* for eight hours a day, Mommy can get so much more done and Bobby can learn his numbers. It's a win-win situation.

After she concedes defeat and embraces the central role of TV in her child's life, a bad mommy can then use it to her advantage to control her children: if they don't eat dinner, then no TV; if they fight with their siblings, then no TV. TV addiction is the gift that keeps on giving!

If you are having friends with children over, great! Go to the computer first and download some hot animated title. With a little luck, the entire brood will be transfixed and won't interrupt Bad Mommy's dinner party for hours. Going on a trip? Strap a portable DVD player on the back of your seats and, aside from bathroom breaks, you may literally never have to interact with your young again.

Once you have accepted the inevitable TV in your home, the video game is not far behind. This wonderful invention and its subsequent addiction will allow Bad Mommy years of freedom from caring for her young. Her children will be safe yet harmless while they stare vapidly for hours into a box, their thumbs and forefingers a flash on the keypad (great for honing those fine motor skills!). A bad mommy knows to accept and embrace the inevitable fact that TV and video games are not the enemy, rather they are a strong weapon in her mommy arsenal.

Before her two children were born, forty-two-year-old Colleen envisioned a strict control of television time: "half an hour a day, only educational, something like *Sesame Street*." At this, Colleen falls into hysterical laughter. Her battle with the dreaded tube has definitely been lost. Or maybe her inner bad mommy has won.

Colleen remembers the day she succeeded in getting her son to finally sit through an entire episode of *Teletubbies*. She and her husband high-fived each other, ecstatic about this brief respite from their son's usual infant routine, i.e., ripping the house apart. "Then, of course," admits Colleen, "the addiction starts." Soon, he was getting videos out of the library—they're educational!—and playing for hours on the computer—it's great for eye-hand coordination! For the month before she gave birth to her second child, her first was virtually "jacked in" to the TV or computer all day. "His only choices were TV or computer for hours and hours, three- to four-hour stretches, only pausing to feed him." A true bad mommy moment.

Now that Colleen has two children, the demand for videos, games, and TV has doubled. The amount of TV watching in her home varies from "zero to appalling. TV allows me to function. I can corral my children safely while I'm doing my own stuff: housecleaning, sleeping, or entertaining," Colleen says. "I feel lazy when they watch TV. If they had a good mommy, they could be in a stimulating activity. It is such bullshit. The truth is that it's easier for me to have them watch TV."

Pascal, a thirty-eight-year-old mother of two girls aged nine and six, freely admits, "Yes, I do use TV as a babysitter." Pascal has gone over to the "other side." She sees TV as a potential friend in her career as a mommy. "TV helps us all to relax," she says. She does express some minor concern with her children's amount of TV watching, admitting, "I don't know what brain cells are ruined." Pascal has a daily TV watching limit in her mind. "I try to limit it, but they wear me down...they know I'm vulnerable at around four in the afternoon—the witching hour. I don't have the will to fight them."

Pascal is not happy about the amount of TV watching going on in her home. "I try to control it, but it doesn't work." TV is a complicated issue. "Without TV, I'd kill them. I'd start spanking. It would be TV or abuse." Pascal wishes it were like the fifties and her children could play outside unattended, but her fear of letting her kids go outside means more TV watching. "They are at least safe when they are hooked in." Their zombie-like faces glued to the flickering of the tube "fills me with peace and horror."

Chapter 23

Crafty Bad Mommy

Very few tasks strike fear into the depths of a bad mommy's heart like organizing a date to do "crafts" with her child (bonus marks for her child and friends)!

Good mommies not only organize a revolving number of crafts to stimulate their child's fine motor skills, hand-eye coordination, and social skills, but find ways to do this in a culturally and environmentally appropriate manner. For example, gathering fallen pine cones for a winter-festival theme or collecting broken robin's eggs to create a spring pastiche of "found art" objects.

Good Mommy has a completely organized craft area, beautifully arranged and colour-coordinated. Her Martha Stewart magazines are full of craft ideas labelled and tagged for future reference. Her children come home from school, excited to find out what theme mommy has planned and how their weekly craft adventure will explore artistic movements and their connection to the environment.

Good mommies dedicate themselves to the art

of child crafts. A good mommy will have at her disposal at least two hot glue guns (large and small), glue sticks, paste (for the little ones), safety scissors for babies, left-handed scissors for the weird ones, and scissors of various shapes for older children. Mommy will need a variety of papers, preferably handmade in her last craft adventure, "making nature-papers from garbage."

A good mommy will invest in a number of pipe cleaners in different colours, sparkles (with and without glue), feathers (different colours, all gathered from nature), dried seeds, cleaned seashells (of non-endangered sea creatures), sand (from the beach, but boiled and bleached to remove toxins), pressed flowers and dried leaves, miniature dried seaweeds, or whatever kind of nature-based ephemera Good Mommy can gather with her darling cherubs.

Bad Mommy is not quite up to snuff in the craft department. Her craft area is a mishmash pile of papers; abandoned, half-missing craft kits; and dried, spilled glue and paint. Because of her internal failure at crafting and lack of energy and joy in the shared craft adventures of her young, her children will never develop their inner craft selves. They will fail miserably at scrapbooking, crocheting, and other important womanly arts. Their ability to socialize with friends over an appropriate activity will be lost and their only option will be sharing a crack pipe with their homies. Without the basic grounding in the art of crafts, her child will be everlastingly divorced from the female arts. You will not only be failing your child, but womankind entirely as yet another generation of children turns their back on the mysteries of the glue gun and appliqué kit, Bad Mommy.

Bridget, a forty-two-year-old mother of a girl, seven, and a boy, four, knows well the shame of craft inadequacy. As a busy working professional, she hardly has the time or inclination to get involved in massive craft projects. "I'm useless: I give them a scrap of paper, some broken crayons." Bridget has a friend who is a true good craft mommy, who regularly illustrates Bridget's failure in this area. "The woman has seasonal displays up in her windows; she's that kind of woman." Bridget's children frequently beg to go to this friend's home. On their last play date with this friend, they made corn-husk dolls. Corn-husk dolls! They actually hand-formed dolls out of corn husks.

Bridget is in awe. "This woman has feathers; she has sprinkles, sparkles, and different scissors that cut different shapes...did you know there are different scissors that cut different shapes?" Bridget says, "It's a particular kind of personality that does this sort of thing...this is fun for them...there are books for these people in the library, apparently." Bridget claims that the litmus test for a good craft mommy is whether or not they own a label maker. "If there is a professional label maker in the home, you have lost: you can't compete with that!"

Kathleen, a forty-one-year-old mother of a nine-year-old boy, fully admits to her own craft inadequacy. "I just don't have an overwhelming desire to do crafts with my child." Surrounded by legions of stay-at-home moms with fully articulated craft projects, Kathleen is a rebel who says proudly, "No one did crafts with me; I just don't feel the impulse." Kathleen admits that the only crafting done in her home is "at the instigation of my husband." Her husband, a stay-at-home dad, picks up the craft slack. "It's nice to have him compensate for my inadequacy...but there is guilt that I have neither the desire, nor need, nor ability to take it on," reflects Kathleen. "Dad is the so-called mom. That's why I'm the bad mommy."

Kathleen knows there are no free rides for a bad mommy. "It's mixed. I'm happy my son gets to do stuff, but I wonder what he will say, as an adult, about my role in his childhood." Her sister-in-law is a craft maven, surrounded by things she has found and crafted from markets. "I think, wow, she's got a lot of time on her hands. It must be nice."

Chapter 24

Bad Mommy and Toys

To the childfree person, the relationship between toys, children, and their mommies appears to be straightforward. Children want to play with toys, they badger their mommy to purchase them, and the toys are purchased, played with, and then discarded.

In reality, the situation is much more complicated. A quick visit to Toys "R" Us is not for the faint of heart. One is besieged with rows after rows of plastic dollies and vaguely menacing fake weaponry. It is an overwhelming selection of packaged bling. Which toy should Good Mommy buy? Which one will stimulate her little angel's latent interest or skills setting them up for a life of success? Which one will stimulate her sweetie's violence centre, setting them up for a lifetime of failure? Which one is on sale?

Bad Mommy doesn't buy toys to make her children happy, she buys toys to distract her children from their never-ending demands on her for stimulation so that she can (selfishly) have some time and energy left for herself. Make no mistake; the toy is merely an instrument for Mommy to avoid having to interact with her child—the more engrossing and addictive the toy, the better. Hence, the incredible popularity of immersive activities, such as video games, with parents. Once your child is hooked, you have complete domination over them, with minimal time spent on actual parent-child engagement.

Aside from video games, which will ruin our children's ability to develop social skills and give them early myopia, there are many other ways to mommy poorly with toys. For example, you can easily manipulate and destroy your child's burgeoning sense of sexual identity through toy choice. Buy little Annie a dolly and you are embracing the patriarchal hegemonic ideology that females must nurture small creatures. Don't buy her a dolly and you will be missing the critical sensitization period of her life where she learns to love and nurture, leading her to likely not have children (and robbing your mitochondrial DNA its opportunity to continue to replicate and manifest itself in future generations). The lack of dolly exposure as a child might even lead her to mommy poorly—one might even say badly—as an adult! This is true particularly if you have selfishly denied her the joy of a younger sibling. How else will she learn this significant task?

This dilemma is also found with boys and weapon toys. Buy Christopher a dolly and you might as well tape a "kick me" sign to his back, since you'll be dooming him to a childhood of ridicule and bullying. Buy him a toy gun and seal your fate in Bad Mommy Hell as he menaces the neighbourhood with his weapon, proudly telling the other local lads that his "Mommy lets him have it." Bad mommies who actually allow gun-type toys in their homes know in the pit of their stomachs that someday this choice will come back to haunt them, hopefully not literally!

Many first-time mommies swear to the Mommy Gods that they will not allow weapon toys in their home. They are short-sighted and wasting their important prayer points; they will quickly learn this is an impossible battle to win. With some children, anything is a potential weapon. Toast can be chewed into the shape of a gun! The letter L and the number 7 fridge magnets—seemingly innocuous—when turned on their sides are also guns! Take away these and the trusty forefinger and thumb will come in handy for a little weapon-play at the kitchen table! Aside from amputation, there is very little you can do to stop a weapon-obsessed child from finding a weaponesque item to play with.

Should Mommy fight to curtail this instinct, it will go underground and manifest itself later in the teen years as her child joins some gang of misfits and mentally ill youth to foment designs to blow up a high school (most likely wearing trench coats or all-black Goth ensembles).

The joy of toys doesn't end here! If you purchase a toy made of plastic, what is it doing to the environment? Where will it go once it is no longer interesting? The landfill? What do you think happens to all those tiny little pieces of plastic that break off children's toys? A bad mommy knows these "chokies" will end up lodged in the trachea of a visiting toddler before you can say "dial 911." What third-world child was exploited to bring you a $4.99 action figure? You know it's your child's karma that will suffer because of your toy choice, Bad Mommy!

Some Mommies eschew all mass-made toys and focus their toy purchases on wooden, handmade toys, optimal for encouraging their child's development. Mommies, be warned! This is a trap too! The wood used for making these wholesome toys was probably first growth (bad tree karma), or infested with pine beetles, which will crawl out of your toys at night, taking over your neighbourhood and ruining all trees in sight. At best, these toys will be painted (by exploited third-world children) with lead paint that your child will chew and ingest, resulting in permanent brain damage.

Best bet: throw away the toy and give them the box. That's what they really wanted in the first place anyway.

Forty-two-year-old Bridget is a professional and a "good feminist." Before children, she was completely committed to a "genderless childhood." She planned a "Barbie embargo" before the birth of her first child, a girl. This resolve faded quickly as Bridget learned that children are social creatures. Although her daughter engaged in some gender-free play at home, she came home from daycare with tales of a friend who would not play with her unless she wore a dress. Bridget says "indoctrination happens early whether you like it or not." Bridget's daughter became focused on all things pink and all things "girl." Her daughter's room is full of Barbies.

Bridget is still holding out on the issue of violent toys. Her four-year-old son is attracted to all things stereotypical of boys. Bridget still "won't cave on guns" and hopes this embargo lasts. Her son creates guns out of pieces of dried spaghetti, anything he can get his hands on. If he thinks she is watching him, he will refer to his gun as a "magic love stick," but both she and he know the reprehensible truth. Bridget tries to explain her hatred of gun toys to her son. "Guns aren't friendly," she explains, to which he solemnly promises (fondling his "gun"), "I won't be 'biolent,' Mommy."

Pascal, the mother of two girls aged six and nine, lives in a Barbie world, much to her horror and dismay. Her mother-in-law is a shopaholic and has purchased two sets of every imaginable pink Barbie item possible so that each child will have her own set. Thus, Pascal is besieged by two complete sets of Barbie condos, cars, furniture, and "little bits of shit that I have cleaned up so many times it physically makes me sick." Cleaning and organizing this seething pink chaos is almost impossible. "That sound they make in the vacuum, it really bothers me...I really want to sort them." The Barbie mess has taken on a life of its own. "It's the Barbie shackles; these pink plastic arms are grabbing at me."

Pascal has a fantasy: "I'm going to cull, make a big pile of naked Barbies and turn it into some art project in the backyard, all pink arms and legs." Pascal also feels karmic guilt related to her children's toy consumption. "I'm sick of Barbies: they represent plastic, and little exploited Asian kids are probably making them. I'm a pimp of abuse of third-world children." Sometimes when her children are distracted, Pascal wants to "fill up a bag or two and out it goes...like anyone will miss it."

Chapter 25

Bad Mommy at School

In our own childhoods, it was straightforward for Mommy. We all went to school. We all attended the school in our neighbourhood. In our local school, we would happily mix with our friends, neighbours, and peers who we would grow up with in a cohesive cohort, supporting each other through the trials and tribulations of childhood and into our adult lives.

Nothing so simple could exist now. The education of our young is an anxiety-provoking impossibility filled with hidden pitfalls, traps, and permanent records. Children don't go to the neighbourhood school anymore. Perish the thought! If they attend their local school, they will be exposed to local riff-raff and never feel challenged to rise above the station of their parents. Instead, mommies apprehensively search for schools that are free, yet have a little extra panache. A second-language immersion school, a fine-arts school, or even a charter-school with no grades and children referring to their teachers by their first names—anything but a "school" school!

As a result of the slavish obsession with getting

children into the right school, children no longer attend schools in their neighbourhoods. Arguably, they may be experiencing a slightly superior type of education, but there will be no one to walk home with from school. With school peers from all over the city, these special schools will leave Bad Mommy's child socially isolated and unable to make lasting peer connections.

Once Mommy has located a school that she thinks will meet the needs of her darlings, she then needs to consider what role she will—not may—take in the school. Mommy involvement is mandatory. It is no longer good enough for Mommy to send a box of cupcakes once a month for goody day. Parent Advisory Councils (PACS) and schools are run on the backs of mommy labour. Any bad mommy not pulling her weight is quickly noted, tagged, and systematically hunted down by other members of the PAC. These PAC mommies can send a chill to the depths of a bad mommy's heart. At one glance, they can tell a bad from a good mommy and will not rest until every mommy "volunteers" a minimum of ten hours a week at the school for each child. Even that will not be enough! Car washes, bottle drives, school "carnivals," walk-a-thons, and other grabs for cash will quickly separate the mommy wheat from the mommy chaff, but we know what kind of mommy you are already anyway, don't we?

Some schools thoughtfully have a reading program in which Mommy is expected to sit for twenty minutes every morning in the classroom, reading with her young. This is absurd. Why would a mommy take her child to school to read to them when she could just as easily read at home while drinking a cup of coffee and using the toilet? This type of morning reading program also assumes that Mommy has nothing better to do in the morning, such as, oh, going to work or something silly like that. If Bad Mommy does not participate in this reading program, again, her absence will be noted and her status as the school's pariah parent even better established.

Some mommies (good most likely, though patently insane) choose to home-school their children so that they have more control over the education process and their child's socialization opportunities. The concept of staying home, by choice, every day with school-aged children is beyond comprehension. Children and parents need a break from each other: look at the devastation wreaked by an entire summer off with children! Staying home to teach your young is aberrant and abnormal behaviour and, more important, it makes the rest of us look bad. Home-schooling is just another way to isolate our children from their peers so that they have no sense of typical development of children with the added bonus of not having to get them dressed or pack lunches.

Some mommies feel that no school is up to the standards they set for their children and thus they choose to not school their children at all. "Un-schooling" is a hard-core version of home-schooling, where children are basically left to their own devices. According to un-schoolers, children will learn when they are ready to learn, and they will seek out the appropriate resources themselves. This is the biggest cop-out of all as a mommy and thus deserves special attention from bad mommies. Truly bad mommies can "un-school" and absolve themselves from any responsibility for their children's failure, as their children simply are not ready yet to move towards the next educational level. Sweet.

Star, a thirty-four-year-old mommy of an eleven-year-old, is suffering from a total "disconnect from school." Prior to returning to work full-time, Star was able to take her child to school and pick her up and take part in school-based activities. Star was a real-life PAC Mommy. "PAC mommies are crazy people; they are insane. There are two types, the ones who are there to defend their children from any type of discomfort—ever—and the kind who really needs a job and so take it on like a religion."

Despite the craziness of the other PAC mommies, at least being on the PAC insured Star that she knew what was going on in the school. "If you aren't picking up and dropping off your kid, you know nothing." Now that she is back to work, Star is on the other side. "If you are a working mommy and don't get home until six, what about homework?" She is not able to check in with the teacher daily and make sure that assignments are finished or brought home.

Star's daughter is not succeeding like she would hope academically. Star admits, "She's probably not the easiest child to teach." Her daughter "loses everything" and is "exceptionally disorganized." Star doesn't know if it is the school's fault or hers. "Kids of bikers are going to that school. How is she going to get ahead?" Star will "flip out" about her daughter getting Cs on her report card, but as a working mommy, what is she going to do about it?

After spending eleven years in private Catholic schools herself, Pascal wanted her two children to go to their neighbourhood school—a shocking and radical concept. Friends were researching cross-boundary special schools, French schools, and art schools. Pascal briefly considered some local schools with more panache but ultimately conceded defeat. "I'm lazy. Driving them to school was just not going to happen!" Pascal doesn't ask for much as a school parent and feels that this is her key to success. "Be kind and respectful to my kid, that's all I'm asking. I'm happy."

Pascal tries to be a low-maintenance parent. She "can't handle the over-involved parents," and prefers to be a hands-off mommy. Her low profile extends into the home. Pascal says that she doesn't "do homework with them after school. I admit I'm kind of lazy that way." Pascal had a first-hand experience being a PAC mommy. She quit because she "couldn't stand the politics...I couldn't handle another fucking meeting." After this near brush, she now avoids the volunteer scene as much as possible: "When I walk past the volunteer board, I look the other way." When the notices for PAC events come home from school, they "go straight into the recycling; I won't even read them."

Chapter 26

Extracurricular Bad Mommy

It's all really Tiger Woods' fault. The story goes that his parents started him golfing at age two. At age two! They put a tiny little golf club in his tiny little hands and started regular practicing. How did they know to do this? What would have happened if they had chosen another sport or a later date or an art or cello lessons? Parents like them make it impossible for the rest of us.

Truly gifted people start practicing and embracing their lifelong gift at a very young age. If this window of opportunity is missed, the gift will never develop in the way it was intended, and an opportunity will be gone for good. It is Mommy's job (of course) to bring together youngster and gift-creating opportunities in an omniscient swami-like manner.

Organizing your children's lessons can be a real nail-biter. Of course, there are the obligatory swimming lessons, gymnastics, and karate. Children need art lessons and a basic grounding in at least one musical instrument. The choices are unbelievable, and how are you supposed to know which one is the right fit?

Most children with at least passably good mommies attend a minimum of three extracurricular lessons a week. A good mommy knows it is all-important to find the right balance in this holy trinity of activities: one must nurture the body, the second should encourage the artistic nature, and the third activity should speak to the social nature of the child. For example, gymnastics, piano, and Guides could be an acceptable trio.

This teetering balance of classes and timetables needs to fit around actual school, other siblings' similar schedules, sleep, food, homework, and—oh—Mommy's job (how could we forget that?). Should a mommy actually find the right balance of lessons, she need not fear, the lessons will change every three months as their session providers juggle their schedules. Just as little Amy's marimba lessons pick up, they will be replaced by Sally's tai chi classes.

One must never vary from this time-tested formula. Heaven forbid you be the bad mommy who (in a Tiger Woods–inspired guilt attack) enrolls her child in more than the requisite three events. Should you do this, you will be overextending your child and not allowing them the all-important free time to develop their sense of play and autonomy. A child's extracurricular needs are a fine balance, easily ruined by an under- or over-zealous Bad Mommy.

Another factor to consider when enrolling

children in lessons is the cost and availability. Most lessons occur right after school on the weekday. Hence, if you are a working bad mommy with children in after-school care, this isn't going to happen. Second, these lessons are brutally expensive. Any type of personalized attention can send Mommy into bankruptcy. It's not unheard of to spend $800 to send two children for swimming lessons at a semi-private swimming centre (where, of course, all future Olympians started their swimming lessons). A third barrier to extracurricular success is simply timing. If a mommy has more than one child, she is managing an exponential number of lessons. Of course, her children could not take the same lesson simultaneously, as this would not allow her children to develop their self-sufficiency separate from their siblings. Hence, this juggling act of lessons will need to be masterminded and will likely involve spread-sheets in order to consider each child's needs separately

Some bad mommies are overwhelmed by this rigorous task and eschew all extracurricular activities in response, preferring to let the needs of the child be met in the classroom or by the family. These neglectful bad mommies have doomed their children. What if wee little Tiger Woods' mommy had decided that golf lessons were not necessary? Would he be working at McDonald's now?

As a first-time mommy, Star was anxious to get her child enrolled in classes—and early. "Every time I entered her in anything, I'd have fantasies that she would be the best." Star enrolled her daughter in everything, and her daughter simply refused to participate. The more anxious Star would be about extracurricular success, the more her daughter would balk. "I've met my match in my daughter," says Star. Her daughter failed the first level of swimming three times, refusing to even touch the water. Star kept on trying, and her daughter kept on rejecting her suggestions. Every endeavour was briefly attempted then rejected: Brownies was "lame"; soccer was also rejected, since "they kick at you in the rain"; in basketball, they just "throw the ball at your head"; in skating, you wear "uncomfortable shoes and cheesy outfits"; volleyball makes your arms "hurt"; and in baseball, you get "hit in the face with the ball."

Star's daughter is currently attempting choir to appease her mother: "I told her, you have to join choir. Kids who don't participate in activities are under the bridge, smoking dope...she said, 'I won't be under the bridge smoking dope, I'll be out on the street corner drinking alcohol.'"

Star is aware that she has failed. She has a "good mommy" friend whose children are all in the regimented three activities each. "Even though her kids are little, they are in ballet, judo, and violin, at age three...age three! This is a sequin-sewing-on type of mommy," Star explains. "She's always driving those kids everywhere and always with snacks packed in advance. I hate her!"

When Pascal, a thirty-eight-year-old mother of two girls, aged nine and six, had her first child, it was all "by the book" in terms of activities—swimming, music, you name it. Pascal learned very quickly that she had a "spirited child" who didn't take to early structure. Her first failure was at an "Academy of Music" at age three. Pascal thought: "She's musical; I just know it in my heart," but her daughter was not appropriate for the academy, as she refused to take part in her first big concert. Pascal then moved her focus to piano lessons, but the teacher told them it wouldn't work out. Pascal admits they "needed more time to work on real things, like reading and writing, not extracurricular."

The tide has turned for this bad mommy: "I don't care anymore." Her second child has tried several different classes but is fickle and changes her mind weekly. "She gets bored easily, and I'm not the kind of parent with the patience to just sit there." Pascal is not investing the energy to push her children. "Sometimes kids just need to be left to play. What's so wrong with that? I look at the list of activities and I laugh. Are all these parents really willing to support their child for the rest of their lives?"

Pascal thinks the whole notion of organized extracurricular activities is a farce. "Why can't kids just be kids until they are fourteen? Why can't they just hang out?" Children who are overly programmed "are going to be exhausted by the time they enter university."

Chapter 27

Discipline and Bad Mommies

Children are naughty and mommies get angry. Very angry. This is a fundamental human truth. When we are angry, we are not able to make good choices. When your blood pressure is high and your heart is beating rapidly, you are not in any position to consider what kind of "gentle language" to use to approach a "teachable moment." Bad Mommy knows what she should do in response to naughtiness, but she also knows what she does do, and the two are rarely one and the same.

When we feel stress, there is a part of our brains that elicits the "fight or flight" response. As mommies are not allowed "flight" (without becoming really bad), the only option under duress is to "fight." Trying to have a fight with a two-year-old is pointless, and the most well-intentioned mommy will find herself trying to reason heatedly with someone who still wears diapers. It's amazing how quickly even the most reasonable conversation with a difficult child can start to become verbally abusive. Verbal abuse, so easy to do, is perhaps the most harmful type of abuse to a child. Those poisonous threats whispered to a child in the hallway at school underneath a fake mommy-smile will never be forgotten and will form the basis of countless therapy sessions as adults.

If and when reasoning does not work, many mommies resort to "time outs." The purported reason for this is to give everyone some time to cool down. The real reason for this is to get the child out of arm's reach of their bad mommy. Time outs may work in some circumstances but are limited by the environment. You can't give a time out in the car, for instance. As well, for many children, sending them away will only worsen the situation. Some anti-social children like being alone. Your child will stop turning to people for comfort and will become a loner who spends all their time by themselves in their rooms, devising ways to blow up their high school, all because of judicious overuse of the time out in childhood.

Physical discipline, a.k.a. "beating," children is out of vogue, although who can deny the desire to pummel a naughty child? Spanking a child for biting, hitting, kicking, and being anti-social will really drive home what kind of a hypocrite you have become. Hitting your children only teaches children that hitting is an option. Furthermore, children will then proceed to share this important hitting lesson with any adult they come into contact with, resulting in a child protection investigation of your home. If you hit your children, there is a good chance that someone will come and take your children away from you for a very long time. We are bad mommies, not criminal mommies, so physical discipline, the beloved, time-tested technique of our own childhoods, is no longer an option for parenting. Sigh.

Some mommies, realizing that verbal and physical consequences are not viable options, turn to a system of rewards and punishments known as a "token economy." Children will have charts on the fridge with little checks for good behaviour and an X for naughtiness. When the child receives a certain number of checks, they will be rewarded with their desired treat. Although this idea works in theory, the discipline needed to actually stick to one of these charts for more than three days is beyond the scope of most bad mommies. The half-abandoned charts sticking to the fridge are just further testimony to your failing long battle with discipline, both with your children and with your bad mommy self.

No matter what type of discipline Bad Mommy chooses to use with her child, her child will be irreparably harmed. Should she over-discipline and embrace a parent-centred approach, her children will become damaged and abused little fragile flowers with no sense of ego integrity and a lifelong need for intensive analysis and, most likely, problems with substance abuse. Should Bad Mommy choose the high road and allow child-centred parenting (i.e., no discipline), her children will run her into the ground. With no boundaries and no direction, they will become damaged and abused little fragile flowers with no sense of ego integrity and a lifelong need for intensive analysis and, most likely, problems with substance abuse. As well, in both cases, the child, when grown, will then proceed to parent her children in the same way and blame it all on Bad Mommy, as that was the way she "was parented."

Colleen is a forty-two-year-old mother of a nine-year-old son and six-year-old daughter. Colleen says, "The overriding feature of my failure as a mommy is my use of empty threats...look up 'empty threats' in the dictionary and there you will see a picture of me." Colleen and her futile words are completely unrealistic, and her children know it: "They are playing us like violins." She will threaten her children with humdingers such as "no presents at Christmastime" or "leaving a holiday on the first day...it's ridiculous."

Before having kids, Colleen envisioned herself using logical consequences and appropriate, consistent teamwork. However, now she threatens, yells loudly, and swears: "Nice." Colleen likes to think that she has a great dirty look, but her children often just turn their heads and look the other way. Colleen feels that "threats and consequences with children are like a big game of chicken." She simply "doesn't have the staying power to wait it out. They win." Colleen appreciates that she is not alone in this struggle: "I smile when I see mommies yell at their kids in the store." Colleen feels like her options are running out. "Do I just wait for them to grow up and leave?"

As a forty-year-old mother of two teens, Krissy admits that discipline for her is a combination of "threats and bribes." When her children were younger, she did attempt "physical discipline, translation: spanking" on a couple of occasions. "Yes, it was kind of satisfying for like a microsecond, then the horror kicked in." Krissy finds it fascinating that her children seem to have no recollection of this actually happening. She isn't in a hurry to correct them, as it will "probably come out in some repressed memory therapy in their thirties anyway."

Krissy's dad was a child behaviourist when she was a girl, so she is well acquainted with the idea of behaviour modification, and at various times in her life, her family fridge has been adorned with little charts and stickers. Krissy understands the basic idea of behaviour modification but notes, "It was a dismal failure for us, perhaps because we all forgot about it and stopped filling in the charts after a couple of days."

These days, Krissy threatens to "take away the cellphone or computer. Those are the big guns." The removal of immediate online contact with friends is a much bigger threat than a spanking ever was. Even that's a "little bit of a sham," she admits. Krissy often will remove a privilege for "at least a month, but they know that's a crock. By tomorrow, it will be down to three days—at most."

Although she used to decry parents who spoke roughly to their children, Krissy admits she is a "screamer." This bad mommy "swears like a sailor" at her kids and "yells the truly most inappropriate things you could ever imagine." She purposely lives in a single family home because she "doesn't want neighbours to hear the yelling." Basically, Krissy's kids are "in charge of the house and themselves." It's easier having roommates than children.

Chapter 28

Bad Mommy Goes to Hell

The nurturing of your wee child hardly ends with meeting their physical needs. As mommies, we are also responsible for the spiritual growth and well-being of our progeny, not to mention their everlasting place in eternal damnation or eternal bliss. No small charge here!

Religion is a tricky one. Get it right and we all win (maybe), get it wrong and we are all doomed (maybe).

If Mommy was raised in a particular faith and practices it in her home regularly, and if, perchance, her partner is also from the same faith and also practices it regularly, it would seem fairly obvious that their child would be brought up in the same way and would practice the same way. Nothing could be so simple though, could it? Isn't this like putting all your eggs in the same basket? What if the particular religion that they all practice is wrong? Then what? Eternal damnation for all, Bad Mommy! As well, by pushing her own beliefs on her unsuspecting children before they are old enough to make their own decisions, Mommy is robbing her young of free will. If they don't come to a faith by choice, does it really count? Likely not. Eternal damnation again for all!

What if Mommy and her partner are both religious, but are from different religious backgrounds? Will their child go to two different hells for eternal damnation or just one? Perhaps you can send your child to both religious types of training: church on Sunday and synagogue on Saturday. Your child will undoubtedly thank you for this confusion and intrusion on their precious spare time. As well, hedging your bets in this manner is not a "get-out-of-eternal-hell-free card." Most religions do not look kindly upon this spiritual double-dipping, and it's still eternal hell for all.

Should Mommy be a person who doesn't practice any religion who still sends her child for religious training even though she herself does not go (you know who you are), you are known as the Hypocrite Bad Mommy. Many hypocrite bad mommies choose this option, thinking that at least their child will go to heaven and God might look favourably upon Mommy's own life circumstances, given that their child's soul was handed over. Does Mommy really think this is going to wash? How is she going to explain to her child how important religious instruction is if it isn't important to her? Children see through this sort of lie by about age seven. Her child will either decide to join her in her disdain or will try to save her soul, thinking that Mommy is clearly going to hell (probably true). Either way, Mommy has set one hell of an example, so to speak.

You smug atheists mommies can wipe the smiles off your sinning faces right now. Do you really think the majority of this world's population has really got it so wrong? Just because there is no proof of the existence of God doesn't mean "He" doesn't exist. By not ensuring that your child has a good grounding in religion, you bad atheist mommies (sinners) are everlastingly cursing your child, and likely the generations to follow, to a life of godlessness and, of course, burning in everlasting damnation afterward. At least children of atheists will have their bad sinner mommies for company, which is a small solace.

Scarlett, a mommy of two, considers herself to be a "thoughtful Christian." Raised by Catholic parents who lapsed in her early childhood, Scarlett was taken to Sunday school by neighbours "who took me along because they were concerned for my soul." She has had a difficult path back to God, which came through the birth of her first child. At the very moment of birth, she says she felt the "touch of God on my head" and she knew she had to do something about it.

For months, Scarlett agonized over what to do. Her husband is "profoundly anti-religious," and Scarlett didn't have a lot of direction or support to find her path to God. "I don't have the time, I'm a new Mommy, and I can't sort it out," Scarlett admits. "I felt like a religious cop-out. I didn't have time to figure out what the right church was, so I returned to the church of my childhood." Scarlett doesn't have a lot of support from her husband to attend church. "If I were training for a marathon on Sunday mornings, he would be very supportive, but this doesn't have any value to him."

Scarlett baptized both of her children to her husband's dismay. "Why did we have to do that?" he asked. Scarlett sees this baptism as a "safety net": at least they are protected (maybe) should something go wrong. This schism between her husband and Scarlett is confusing to the children. Last week, their daughter asked: "Daddy, why don't you go to church with us?" Scarlett says, "I felt like muttering under my breath, 'Because he's a faithless human being.'"

Annie, a thirty-six-year-old mother, has a complex history with religion. Her dad was an Anglican and her mother was a Catholic, and together they raised their children as born-again Christians. Out of this background, Annie has found herself being a staunch atheist. She pretty much rejects all types of religion: "I can't walk past a church without wanting to spit on it. I hate religion." To further complicate the issue, her husband's parents are "hard-core" Buddhists.

Although her husband is mostly staying out of the religious debate in the home, their eight-year-old is showing increasing signs of being "very spiritual." She always goes to temple or church with her grandparents. Annie says, "She asks me if I believe in God, and I tell her that I believe in all religions; that there is good and evil in all religions. I've told her that there is no God as well. I think I kind of mess her up a bit. I'll tell her that there is no God, but then I tell her I hope there is a hell for horribly bad people who I hope will burn in hell, such as George Bush. I don't believe in heaven, but I still believe in hell. I'm worried that I scare the shit out of her."

Although, given her own traumatic background, Annie would prefer her child not be involved in any type of religion, she admits, "Secretly it bugs me that she is drawn to Buddhism, even though I also hate the Christian side." Better the devil you know!

Chapter 29

Bad Mommy Gets It On

It all comes down to sex in the final analysis. If we hadn't had sex, we would not be mommies (for the most part). It's painfully ironic that children, little beings who were created by the very sexual act itself, are the ultimate enemy to healthy sexual expression.

Children seem to have an innate preprogrammed sense of when their mommy is either planning to have sex or is actually engaging in the act. This is likely an evolutionarily adaptive response. A child who senses that the sex act is about to occur will do everything in their power to stop it, thus insuring that a younger sibling does not arrive on the scene to steal resources from the older child; it's a sort of built-in Darwinian birth control.

When your children are too young to develop this uncanny sense (which appears to emerge some time in the first year of life), you will still not be having sex. Enforced insomnia, massive weight gain, potentially squirting boobies, and traumatized nether regions render the average new mommy asexual at best. The last thing Mommy wants to engage in is the act that got her in this mess in the first place.

Should a new mommy unwisely push through her natural desire to refrain from sexual congress in the early months, she and her partner will have to contend with her boobies. It is apparent that mammals, humans included, should not be having sex in the early breastfeeding months. The very act of breastfeeding inhibits vaginal secretions to nil, creating your very own dry gulch. This is clearly a sign from the gods. Should you ignore this and still soldier on despite the impenetrable barrier, you will find that your new-mommy boobies, full of milk, tend to drip or even squirt when sexually aroused. Although this can be amusing for the first time, the spraying milk and fountains of mommy make your bed smell like a yoghurt factory. This cheesy odour is a libido killer.

Once your children have grown up a little and lactation is no longer a pressing concern, there are still many ways to feel uncomfortable with your sexuality as a parent. There are few guarantees that your bed will actually be childfree at night. Even if your child actually sleeps in their own bed (which is far from a given), many children do a nighttime bed migration, and at some point in the night, particularly if awakened by strange sounds, dreams, smells, thoughts, or monsters, they may come creeping into your bed. This *childus interuptus* can be utterly unnerving. Just as the waves of sexual ecstasy start to crest, Mommy will feel a patting on her leg, followed by a hesitant, "Mommmmmyyyyy.....?" That's hot! Bad Mommy and child, scarred for life. For years to come, the vision of their Mommy as a two-headed beast will be a primary theme on the therapist's couch.

By exposing her child to her own sexuality, Bad Mommy will elicit the Electra complex, in which a daughter will fantasize about killing her mother and becoming her father's wife, or the Oedipus complex, in which a son will fantasize about killing his father and becoming his mother's husband. Make no mistake: any discovery of any complex in your child, now and forevermore, will be linked to you, Bad Mommy.

Should you be one of those mommies who truly savours her privacy and waits until the children are either out of the home or under medicated sleep to have sex, your children will be spared the horrors of seeing you in an intimate embrace. However, your children will then not have proper intimacy modelled for them. Children without solid intimacy models will assume that their parents do not have mutually satisfying relationships. For the rest of their lives, they will be doomed to shallow, meaningless, emotionally devoid relationships because of this, you prudish bad mommy.

Really, regardless of your postpartum sex life,

your children will be forever scarred and ruined, so go fiercely into that good night and screw your courage to the sticking place, Bad Mommy. A lock on the door and a little eighties music can go a long way.

Twenty-seven-year-old Kitty is six months pregnant with her third child. She says, "When I'm pregnant, I'm horny; I have the sex drive of a seventeen-year-old boy." Kitty wants "dirty raunchy hotel sex, not nice married sex." She has been married for the last eight years and either pregnant or nursing the entire time. She believes this has caused her hormones to go insane.

Despite her need for sex, Kitty is finding that kids cramp her style. She would like to have sex in the afternoon or in the living room: "Bed sex and 9 p.m. sex are too boring." Kitty believes in a firm and early bedtime for her kids (the true reason for the invention of the early bedtime) or it's "too late and I'm too tired." Kitty has a technique for sneaking in some afternoon sex. She will settle the children with an engrossing DVD and quickly sneak upstairs for some sex.

Kitty knows the key for success is preparation, and she always has a good store of DVDs on hand. Early in her career as a mommy she made her husband get up first thing in the morning to drive to the DVD store so that they could distract the child and have sex. But by the time her child was set up with his DVD, pillows, and snacks, it was too late and she wasn't horny anymore. Kitty's key to sexual success? DVDs and hardwood stairs that make a lot of noise combined with "children who are stompers."

Scarlett, a thirty-six-year-old mommy of two, is still a very sexual being. "[Kids have] definitely cramped my style," begins Scarlett. As her children are now seven and ten, she is finally feeling like she is able to be more sexual. When they were little and nursing, "the kids had fucking radar...the second we got into it, they would wake up, then it was over. I couldn't switch between harlot and caregiver."

Scarlett makes sure she takes care of business now: "I masturbate sometimes. I say to the kids, 'Mommy needs to lie down. Don't bug her for half an hour.' Then I have a little wank. I find it centres me." Scarlett admits that she is bad. She says, "I will leave my kids alone with power tools so I can have a wank." Scarlett finds it a challenge to balance being a sexual woman and being a mommy. She lives with fear of being "caught out" by her children.

Scarlett admits to enjoying "kinky sex" but fears the inevitable conversation with her child when he stumbles under the bed and pulls out forty yards of rope and asks, "What is this for, Mommy?" Scarlett recalls her daughter walking in on her and her husband having sex doggy style and her daughter exclaiming, "Daddy, why are you hurting Mommy?" She thought then: "I need to put some money away for counselling." After this incident, she had locks installed on her bedroom door. She thinks it may be time for some better sound insulation too. "How ironic: they're little creatures created by sex who seem hell-bent to stomp it out."

Chapter 30

Bad Mommy Plays Doctor

"Mommy, I'm not feeling well." These words send a shiver down the spine of any mother. While sick children do have their charm with their strong desire to cuddle and their shiny-eyed maternal devotion, the sick child means that Mommy's life stands still as she transforms into Nurse Nightingale and eschews all other responsibilities and desires.

While there are daddies who claim to care for sick children, this mythic creature is rarely experienced. Late-night vomit, pesky fevers, spots, bruises, headaches, and infected ears all fall squarely on the shoulder of Mommy.

Most mommies will amass a large stockpile of medications, remedies, and the all-important Band-Aids by the time their child is six months of age. These mommies will also have travel versions of their arsenal tucked away in their purses and all the family vehicles. Mommy knows to be prepared or suffer the consequences.

No daycare or school will allow a sick child to stay, which is quite unfair and cruel considering that half the staff typically appear to have the sniffles and/or be under the heavy influence of cold medication at any time. Some mommies have been known to prop up their tot with a heavy dose of medication perfectly timed to wear off as the school day ends, which will reveal the festering mess of infection beneath much too late for anything to be done about it. What's a mommy to do?

Unfortunately, most mommies can't dodge the obvious sickness symptoms and are stuck at home with a sick child. Although some workplaces will allow Mommy to take a day off, not everyone is so tolerant. Finding a friend or family member willing to stay home for free with an infectious child is not as easy as it seems. Most often, Mommy stays home and suffers the wrath of her colleagues at work—another breeder taking time off for her snot-nosed kid.

Mommies are also expected to know how to treat all common childhood illnesses. A painkiller, antacid, Band-Aid, puke bucket, and cold pack in any combination will successfully treat over 90 percent of childhood complaints, but the odd and rare malady may escape Mommy's eagle eye. Woe to the mommy who ignores that little cough only to discover it was pertussis and has infected the entire school. Woe to the mommy who puts a icepack on a sore ear only to learn it was an infected eardrum that has burst and now the child will never hear properly again! Mommy's only option is to take her child to the doctor or clinic for every last medical concern. This will result in medical staff feeling that Mommy suffers from Münchausen by proxy, a mental disorder in which a parent creates an illness in their child for the attention the parent desires. Yes, my friends, that is one hell of a bad mommy.

Sunshine, a thirty-eight-year-old bad mommy of two, admits to deeply detesting caring for her sick children. She feels her children have "virtually no immune systems so to speak" and casually bring home every virus or bacteria with which they make passing contact. Sunshine suspects her children enjoy being home sick so much that they go out of their way to become ill. If at all possible, Sunshine admits she will "prop them up with medication and send them to school anyway. A little Advil first thing in the morning can do wonders." Even though the school will not dispense medications, she gives her children little zip-lock baggies full of Advil and instructs them to take them "at recess or at lunch, but not both"—she's not that bad.

Sunshine feels that the school system is overly punitive to parents, sending children home at the first sign of a sniffle. This is patently unfair, as they "got it from the school in the first place." Sunshine will leave her kids at school unless there is blood or vomit. If she is unable to avoid sending her ill children to school, Sunshine will "take pains to avoid actually interacting with their infected bodily fluids." Her children know where the puke bucket is (under the sink) and they know how to use it. Likewise, snotty tissues need to be picked up by the dispenser of the snot, not Mommy. Sunshine "doesn't do phlegm" under any circumstances. This bad mommy is a strong believer in medication and will "dose at the four-hour point of a four-to-six-hour medication cycle just to make sure."

Despite her deep dislike for caring for sick children, Sunshine will not leave this task to her husband, as he will likely just get infected himself and then be "even worse than the kids could ever be." Sunshine believes that by practicing tough mommy-love, she is preparing her children to be better spouses in adulthood. No one wants to be married to a big snot-nosed baby.

Caring for her sick child makes forty-three-year-old Abigail "as close to a good mommy as I get" explains this mommy of a six-year-old girl. "Sick is pretty hard to fuck up." Abigail's child is generally in very good health and has only vomited twice in her life. The first time her daughter didn't even know what it was and told her parents she was "all wet." It was due to a healthy soaking in vomit.

Abigail is pretty mainstream with her daughter, "I don't even do vitamins. I mean, she has a good diet." Abigail will dose her child with medications if necessary. She can't understand when she hears of children being accidentally overdosed with medications: "That's just stupid. That's like putting Coke in a baby's bottle: if you are too stupid to read the label, you're too stupid to have a baby."

Abigail's daughter is a working actor, and Abigail will dose her with Claritin to "dry her up" if she's a little snotty. Snotty doesn't look good on close-ups. She has also been known to dose with Benadryl for long-haul plane trips, but that's no big secret. Abigail recalls telling her tot on the plane, "It's time for you to go to sleep, so I'm going to drug you now." Abigail's daughter proudly announced after a flight, "It's fine because my mamma drugged me!"

Abigail admits that she has hypochondriacal tendencies herself, so she has to keep this in mind with her daughter and keep it in check. "You don't want to become one of the Münchausen moms," warns this Bad Mommy. Abigail admits to ignoring those "lice letters" that seem to come home monthly from school. If these reports are even somewhat accurate, the entire school system and student body are overrun with vermin. "If she start, really scratching, I'll check. I don't think we need to get all hysterical about it."

Chapter 31

Bad Mommy and Pets

All mommies, good and bad, eventually have to face the pet conundrum at some point in their mommying career. Some mommies had pets before children—in some cases, these pets served as pseudo-children in the relationship. These proto-babies often do not take kindly to being usurped by their younger human siblings. Many a new mommy has faced a steaming pile of cat shit in the baby's crib or a "mystery scratch" on the baby's face. A quick perusal through the pet section of Craigslist will show a lengthy list of cats and dogs needing new homes due to babies being born into the human family. Mommies will often cite "allergies" to make themselves look less neglectful; however, everyone knows that is not the truth. These bad pet mommies have simply tired of their fur babies and moved on to greener pastures.

When the human children grow older, Mommy once again will turn her mind to adding a family pet to the growing and unmanageable roster of her responsibilities. A long-held notion exists in our society that a child needs a dog or cat in order to complete the dream childhood experience. Having a pet will "teach them responsibility" and, in some cases, can serve as a surrogate younger sibling should Mommy not wish to breed again.

Adding a pet to the family can have short-term benefits. While the pet is young and new, it will be amusing and hold everyone's attention. However, the bloom will quickly come off the furred rose, and the pet, like the rest of the toys purchased for the children, will languish, unattended, under the bed. We all know who gets to take care of it forever: that's right—it's Mommy! Despite promises to take the puppy for walkies twice every day and to scoop out the poo box at dusk and dawn, these empty promises from other family members last as long as the dear pet is new.

Should the pet make a long-term adjustment to the family and survive the critical first year, disaster can still lurk around every corner for Mommy. First, children actually do sometimes acquire allergies to pets. This most often will occur just at the point where the entire family has decided that they love this pet and that the family cannot function without this specific animal. The ensuing Craigslist posting and drop off to the SPCA will scar Bad Mommy's child forever, as the lesson that "we get rid of family members who do not fit us anymore" is driven painfully home, or rather, away from home.

Even if no family member acquires an allergy by

some miracle, animals have a nasty habit of dying precipitously—most often just as the children have proclaimed their undying love—and in the most spectacular manner possible right in front of the children, either by being hit by a car or expiring in some other dreadful, grisly fashion. This death will serve to permanently traumatize Mommy's child and will lead to post-traumatic stress disorder symptoms that will manifest themselves throughout the years and harm future relationships with all small creatures.

To avoid this horrendous inevitability, some mommies never allow their children to have pets. These mommies are also, of course, truly bad. By not allowing their child to learn to nurture a small animal, Bad Mommy's child will never know the importance of caring for their own young. This will lead to long-term problems with intimacy and child rearing when their child is an adult. Their child will also not learn to deal with death and process loss, leading to insurmountable trauma when they lose their first human person, as they inevitably will. With no practice pet to grieve on, the child will be in utter shock. As well, by not exposing them to animal dander at a young age, Mommy's child will, of course, develop allergies as an adult, leading the circle of animal torture to continue in yet another generation of a family.

Keira, a fifty-year-old bad mommy of two young adults, has a checkered history with kids and pets. When her daughters were young, she inherited a lovely flame point Siamese cat named Eli. He was a large and friendly cat, and her daughters loved him.

Something was wrong with Eli. He started putting on a lot of weight. One morning, the family awoke to discover Eli had had a litter of kittens in the night. Eli was renamed Elizabeth and the ensuing confusion about "birds and bees" left Keira's children in a semi-permanent state of gender confusion.

Eli/Elizabeth ran away eventually and was replaced by Hoss, a massive and clearly male tomcat. Although the family loved Hoss, Keira decided she needed to get rid of him after he "shat all over my gladiator sandals" and started spraying urine "in retribution for God knows what." She drove him down a long, windy, forested road to a pet cemetery and let him off. "I thought that a nice family would come and bury their dead cat and then, lo and behold, see Hoss standing there in the woods, like an answer to their prayers." After a day and night of feigning ignorance to his whereabouts to her concerned children, Keira returned to the cemetary and found Hoss waiting at the end of the road.

Two years later, in a new relationship and at the insistence of her new partner, who felt that all nuclear families needed a dog, Keira and her family adopted a dog, Luba. Luba was an extremely "high-spirited and barky dog." Alas, Luba was a poor fit for Keira's "avant-garde" lifestyle; the dog's goofiness and frenetic energy were challenging for Bad Mommy Keira. One day, Luba truthfully went missing—"Oh, thank Christ"—and Keira did not go looking for her. No, not at all, despite telling her children that she would. Her children made "missing dog" posters, and Keira feigned putting them up but actually threw them away.

Several weeks later, a new dog showed up in the next-door neighbour's backyard. Keira's youngest daughter, heartbroken by her Luba's absence, realized that this dog was none other than Luba. Keira and her partner agreed to "just ignore her—enough time had passed." She told her daughter, in no uncertain terms, that it "wasn't her! See? It has another name!" Eventually, Keira moved from that neighbourhood to avoid further Luba sightings and confrontations.

Forty-one-year-old Andrea is the mother of a six-year-old boy. Before having children, she and her husband always had cats. Eventually, they decided to "move up the food chain" to dogs, mostly as a test to see whether or not they would be able to handle children: "If we could handle and enjoy a dog, then it would be a good indicator to have a child." Unfortunately, the dog they adopted, an eight-month-old rescue Dalmatian named Jack, was an "extremely inappropriate dog." She likened his adoption to the addition of a "teenaged street kid" into the home, all bad manners and trauma. "It was a bad situation."

Despite the ruination that Jack added to their home with chewing, pooing, and hysterical barking, the family decided to have their own child some years later—after being assured by *Dog Whisperer* types that Jack was not "typical" and thus not a good indicator of their future parenting skills.

Andrea's extended family was concerned about the safety of the baby with Jack, due to his intense prey drive. Andrea actually posed the dog beside the baby "obviously not being eaten" to send to family members. Eventually, thousands of dollars and two years later, Jack succumbed to a blocked urethra and Andrea's husband swore off dogs forever. However, Andrea's uncle bred Chihuahuas, and eventually she, and their now six-year-old son, successfully lobbied for the addition of a new puppy. This one would be small and lovable with a good track record. Her son had complained bitterly of being an only child and, in fact, referred to inanimate objects such as walls and chairs as "Brother Wall" and "Brother Chair" in an attempt to create younger siblings; this new dog would fulfill their child's need.

Diggy, a two-pound Chihuahua puppy, was adopted by the family. Alas, Diggy was too small and delicate for Andrea's boisterous child to play with, so Diggy spent most of his time with Mommy. Diggy now sees himself as Andrea's first child and sees Andrea's birth child as a menace who gets snapped at or growled at if he gets too close to "Diggy's Mommy." Sometimes Andrea feels bad and shoos him off her lap in a show of allegiance to her son. However, as soon as her son is off to school, she and Diggy are reunited. He is her best friend.

Chapter 32

Bad Mommy on a Diet

Every time you open a newspaper or turn on the radio, it's the same story: children are getting fatter and will be the first generation to die younger than their parents. Adults, of course, are getting fatter too, but at least that's only their own fault. Bad Mommy is solely responsible for her child's sky-high BMI and imminent early death—not to mention school-yard bullying due to excessive adipose tissue.

Most mommies feel insecure about their own bodies. This is because childbirth and the ensuing nursing and parenting years take their toll on what might have been—once upon a time—a buff little bod. At some point in her mommy career, Mommy will be told by her doctor or others that she needs to lose weight. As children carefully monitor any behaviour in their parent, the children will quickly pick up on this new-found fetish to monitor carbs and calories. Although Mommy will lie to her children and, of course, tell them that they are beautiful just the way they are, the mixed message sent by Mommy's frequent visits to the bathroom (with tap running, of course) and Costco-sized boxes of protein meal replacement bars tell another story altogether.

Some bad mommies let their own fat fear spread directly to their children, carefully monitoring every bite and scheduling multiple high-cardio exercise opportunities during the week. These mommies instill in their children the knowledge that thin is love and worth, and fat is to be avoided at all times. If Mommy can't love herself when she's fat, how could she ever love her chubby child? Some mommies will claim that their child has "intolerances" in order to better monitor their child's food input. An alarming number of children are now "intolerant" to wheat, making hosting birthday parties with cake more and more of a challenge. There are also children with "blood sugar level issues" who can't engage in sweeteners. Beware the mommy who claims her child suffers from either of these; she is most often using this to cloak her own caloric restrictive obsessions.

Some Mommies give up altogether, both with themselves and with their children. The queen-sized Amazon Bad Mommy and her minivan full of little pumpkins is an increasingly familiar sight at the drive-through window. If Mommy can't control her own desire to hoover through a flat of donuts after a stressful day at the mall, how in the world would she be able to curtail this behaviour in her child? As well, as all mommies know, controlling children's behaviour with food is a powerful tool. Pavlov used dog food with his dogs; mommies use candies and treats with their children. If Mommy robs herself of such a powerful reward system, she might lose all ability to control her young. Fat mommies also enjoy the company of their fat children. By keeping the whole family king-sized, it is clearly a "genetic" issue and not anything to do with gluttony or sloth. Fat Bad Mommy and her chubby daughter can explore the plus-size section of Target together for those darling "little" matching outfits.

Sunshine, a thirty-eight-year-old bad mommy of a boy and girl aged eleven and fourteen, admits to "deep, food-based issues," which have spread to her own children. Although Sunshine knows that a good mommy is supposed to love her children unconditionally, the truth is she winces when she sees them getting fatter, which, unfortunately, seems to happen each week.

Sunshine herself has struggled with an eating disorder for much of her life. She sometimes will do a "cleanse," which is, in reality, an extreme diet, all in the name of "health." Her children regularly see her avoiding carbs and fat like the plague. She also exercises obsessively and can be seen "methodically massaging her fat to break up the fat nodules" when sitting at the family couch.

Several years ago, Sunshine was bulimic. She would prepare a large family dinner and eat several plates' worth. Once the kids were snug in front of the TV and Wii, she would "turn on the radio loudly in the bathroom and crank the taps to cover the splashing sound." A few sprays of bathroom scent and a swig of mouthwash and Bad Mommy was good as new. Sunshine was terribly afraid to be caught and eventually stopped on her own.

These days, Sunshine sees her food issues spreading to her children. Recently, they both were quite sick with the stomach flu. She recalls she was "actually quite happy for the both of them, as the flu's always good for at least five pounds." She admits to allowing her children to eat food that might be slightly spoiled, since a "good bout of diarrhea never hurt anyone." Sunshine has been feeding her children diet soda even though she suspects it's bad for them. She studies the height/weight charts at the doctor's office and holds her breath, hoping that her children will be "height/weight proportionate." She has a BMI calculator on her iPhone with an "adjustable setting for children." Sunshine tries her best but suspects she is failing.

Thirty-nine-year-old Maeve is the anxious mother of a ten-year-old daughter, who she describes as "a strapping girl," and a fourteen-year-old "bean pole of a boy." Bad Mommy Maeve is worried that her daughter is doomed to her same fat fate: "The propensity to fat is there. Look at the gene pool: we're all fat." Maeve admits to her own latent slothfulness: "I'm essentially a lazy person." This has resulted in a life-long battle with fat: "I have an unhealthy relationship with food. It's my best friend and my worst enemy."

Maeve wants it to be known that her daughter, regardless of size, is beautiful "even if she is fat. She'll be the most gorgeous fat girl. She's simply not going to be skinny; that's just not going to happen." Maeve understands that it's a problem with exercise and diet. "I hate exercise. I hate it, but I don't want my kids to hate it." Her plan is to keep her kids active so that no matter what they eat they won't get fat. To this end, her children are in numerous activities throughout the week. Maeve feels exercise is prescriptive: a healthy dose of cardio almost every day will hopefully keep the inevitable fat at bay.

Food is also an issue for this bad mommy: "They love snacking, and they are hungry at all times." Although Maeve monitors what goes on while she is home, her children are sometimes alone by themselves and "God knows what they eat." Maeve is anxious about her daughter getting fat, but she's also anxious about being anxious about her daughter getting fat.

Chapter 33

Bad Mommy Lies to Her Kids

Lying to children is a cornerstone of parenting and one that deserves a high amount of respect. Children must never know what their parents are truly up to or all semblance of control will be lost in the family. The myth of parents who know what they are doing must be protected—at all costs. Children are naturally inclined to believe their parents, which allows parents to exploit this tendency for their own gain.

We live in a cruel and selfish world—that's the truth. Adults hurt children, and adults hurt each other. These are truths that cannot be denied. However, the young child must be shielded from this reality or they will develop deeply neurotic and anxious patterns of behaviour and, most important, they will never move out of the home due to fear. Children must trust that their parents actually know what they are doing so that they will follow, without question, just like little soldiers on the battlefield.

Some mommies pretend that they don't lie to their children. This is a farce! What about Santa Claus and the tooth fairy? These complex and socially accepted lies are the basis of parenting in our society. Mommies happily construct careful lies for their children and, worse yet, expect other family members to condone such behaviour. When the children eventually discover this lie—as they all do—it sets up a lifetime of mistrust between the child and parent. If you were willing to lie about the Easter Bunny, what else are you lying about?

Some lies are more innocent. Parents routinely lie about issues such as their child's appearance (see Bad Mommy on a Diet) in order to shield their child from feelings of low self-esteem. Another favourite area of confabulation involves death or dying (see Bad Mommy and Pets). No one actually "dies," they "go to heaven" or "pass." "Pass into what?" the child might rightly ask.

Mommies lie about their sexuality to their children (see Bad Mommy Gets It On). Children shouldn't be privy to late-night shenanigans between their parents, but some mommies carry this farce a little further, appearing quite chaste in front of their children and denying any past partners, lovers, or husbands. When the inevitable "Where did I come from?" conversation arises, Mommy will be quick to confirm that all of that squeamish behaviour did in fact only occur exactly as many times as there are children in the family. The latch on the top of Mommy's bedroom door is pointedly ignored as something that the previous owners of the house must have had installed for some unknown reason.

Many mommies lie to their children about medical procedures. Taking your child to get their shots, which Mommy knows they will hate, is "just a checkup." What a surprise to everyone when the doctor hauls out the needle that is just "going to pinch a little bit" (another lie).

Bad mommies also love to lie about family breakups. The most common one during a separation from Daddy being that "Mommy and Daddy still love each other very much" (not true, obviously, or they wouldn't be getting a divorce) and that "we are still a family." Again, clearly not, as how can we all be a family with Daddy's new twenty-two-year-old girlfriend and their hated love-spawn replacement child?

It is extremely important that mommies continue to be supported in withholding the truth from their children. Children best learn these sordid truths from their siblings and friends, not their parents. This allows the children to believe that they now know something their parents don't and the circle of lies continues. Little Johnny will hide the porn magazine he and his friend found in an abandoned garage from his parents—whom he believes never have sex except for procreation—and this is good, as the last thing Mommy wants is an actual, frank conversation with her own child about his burgeoning sexuality. Ignorance is truly bliss; the lies that Mommy tells her children, and the lies that her children in turn tell Mommy, preserve this beautiful balance for all.

As a thirty-eight-year-old bad mommy of seven, Suzanne gets very little time together to be intimate with her husband. They generally wait until two in the morning, lock the door, and hope for the best. A few years ago, things apparently got out of hand. The next morning around the family breakfast table, one of the younger children asked why "Daddy was giggling so loud in the night." Apparently, the giggling had woken all of the sleeping children. Suzanne considered her options and felt that this was a good time for Mommy to lie: "Well," she explained, "Daddy actually sleep-giggles. It is similar to sleepwalking, except it only involves giggling. Many people do this!" The children all nodded around the table at this new revelation about their father. Bad Mommy thought nothing more of it, happy to have escaped the truth.

Several weeks later, when the family was entertaining another large family for dinner, Suzanne's husband laughed aloud. Suzanne's youngest child said, "Daddy, you are giggling just like when you sleep-giggle, except that your sleep-giggling usually has a lot of heavy breathing that goes with it!" The child then went on to imitate the combination of loud, sensual breathing and high-pitched giggling to the horrified dinner guests.

The "sleep-giggle" lie has completely gotten out of control and was most recently brought up at a Christmas dinner in front of over thirty relatives. Suzanne and her husband "just want to die," but can't think of a way out of this little lie.

Abigail, the forty-three-year-old mother of a six-year-old, feels that "lies have a place as a parenting tool." She has a wonderful solution for getting rid of jack-o'-lanterns and gingerbread houses at the end of the season. Abigail has informed her daughter that "the jack-o'-lanterns are made into pumpkin soup by Santa's elves to build up their strength for Christmas and the gingerbread houses are used as temporary homes during the Christmas gift-making season—also by the elves." Abigail's daughter fully believes this mythos. Abigail's daughter made a red-crayoned note to go with the gingerbread houses stating: "This is for you, elves." When Abigail's daughter sees pumpkins on neighbours' porches the week after Halloween, she will grimly nod and say, "The elves must not have picked those up yet."

Bad Mommy has come up with a clever way of dealing with the pesky "wrapping paper issue" at Christmas. Abigail is aware that several mommies have been caught in possession of the same wrapping paper as "Santa." Abigail places fabric bags under the Christmas tree on Christmas Eve and explains to her daughter that "Santa brings presents unwrapped and then wraps them when he gets here. Santa likes to recycle and is happy to use the same bags over and over again."

Abigail is not at all worried or feeling guilty about lying to her child. She believes that children are capable of believing and not believing at the same time. Deep down she suspects that her daughter knows there is no Santa, as her child is a "little cynic and is analytical already."

However, her daughter will cite evidence for Santa's existence: "The gifts, the letter in response to her letter, the nibbled carrots, cookies, and the empty beer." Santa is safe in this household, at least for the time being.

Chapter 34

Bad Mommy and Sports

Sports are good! They provide exercise, team spirit, and maybe a chance at being in the Olympics! Every parent secretly hopes that their child will find their true passion and skill in some sport and fulfill (generally Daddy's) desires for a homegrown sport hero.

Sports are expensive! Unfortunately, children grow, like ALL the time, and need their sports equipment in their current size for that month. Some parents attempt to scrimp on this and "make do" for two seasons (an epic fail, as their child will clearly be in flood pants with chaffing equipment) or will attempt to save by purchasing on consignment (also an opportunity for failure, as everyone knows second-hand sport equipment is always infested with athlete's foot or some other unknown and highly infectious microbe).

Sports are also terribly inconvenient for a bad mommy. Most tend to take place at absurd hours, such as five in the morning or ten at night, and most often take place in the most inconvenient weather possible—horrible rain, torrential wind, or in some nasty, unheated arena. Bad Mommy not only needs to take her child and all of their friends to the sporting event de jour, but also stay and brave the elements and—even worse—feign interest and support.

Often, Mommy will also be roped into being a "team parent" and provide extra support to the team…like driving three days a week at five in the morning isn't showing enough support. These "team parents" are also expected to lead in fundraising activities, which are the bane of any parent's existence. After approaching all family and friends to purchase raffle tickets and chocolate bars, or taking part in a fundraiser once, each additional request is just more and more mortifying. Many mommies secretly provide the needed funds out of their own pockets to avoid the mortification but also the shame of being outed as "not being a team player."

Sports often involve travel. Bad Mommy has two choices: either go along as a chaperone and spend her only free weekends and nights with a bunch of drunken horny teens sneaking around cheap shared hotel rooms or let her child go on their own and perhaps be preyed upon by lecherous individuals looking for vulnerable children with no adult chaperone.

Sports are also dangerous! Many children are injured through sports, which can range from a mild sprain to a hospitalization. Many a mommy has sat waiting in the hospital's emergency room while she cradled her burgeoning little sports star's head in her lap. There's nothing like getting an early jump on that rotator cuff injury!

While the media tells Mommy that her child must be active to avoid weight gain, and Mommy also knows that having her child in sports will increase their chances of having friends and escaping bullies, the personal cost in mommy hours is huge. While some mommies will have the payoff of a true sports hero in their home, most will escape the childhood sport years with concussions, minor frostbite, and a drawer full of team photos.

Thirty-nine-year-old Maeve, mother of a fourteen-year-old boy and ten-year-old girl, wasn't raised in sports: "My parents were intellectuals," she says.. As a result, she was "never athletic and paid for it with a weight problem." This Bad Mommy wasn't going to allow this fate to happen to her own children. "No matter what," she swore to herself, "my children are going to be active." Luckily, she married a man obsessed with Little League and swimming. Thank goodness her husband likes swimming so much that he takes their children into the water at least once a week, which Maeve says "is great because, honestly, it's always something for me: I'm not feeling right, I've got to pick up something at the store, I'm getting my period, whatever; Mommy does not want to get into that damn water."

Maeve sees swimming lessons as an enforced exercise program, which will hopefully help to manage her children's weight. When her husband suggested the family sign up for Little League, Maeve was fully supportive. "Did I know how much fucking time I would spend in Little League? NO!" says this bad mommy emphatically. "Little League is every single weekend for the season and one or two nights per week. And let's not forget the parent duties—like paying fees and showing up isn't enough!"

Weekends were a complete write-off for the entire family for months at a time. Maeve was "coerced" into selling chocolate bars to raise funds. "I was too lazy to sell them and just ate all forty of them." As the "Team Parent" married to the "Head Coach," Maeve suddenly had twenty more children: "I was in charge of uniforms, volunteers, emails, trophies, snacks, and field prep. How the fuck did this happen?"

Maeve explains that despite her families' high level of sports involvement, they were "relative light weights. There are families out there who live completely for this stuff. They are on the governing boards or go to the national levels. Now that's just crazy." Luckily, her children are no longer doing Little League. Her daughter is involved in "drop off and pick up sports" such as soccer and dance. They are expensive and involve a lot of driving and cardio, "but no damn participation from Mommy." Thank God.

As a forty-nine-year-old mother of two young adults, Bad Mommy Helen admits she "just hated the pressure, but more important, the other parents" involved with her children's sports. Helen was "totally athletic" herself as a child and encouraged her children to get involved in sports but feels that sports were not designed for working mommies. "Everything always started at six. Who can do that?" Helen was perpetually ten minutes late with her kids. "I just hated all the parents, especially the ones who were really into it and gave me the evil eye for being late. Sorry, some of us work."

Despite everything, Bad Mommy was always late for practice and was thus ostracized by the other parents or forced to stand beside the really obnoxious mommies on the field: "Oh my God, I just wanted to slit my wrists whenever I was trapped beside these awful, loud-mouthed know-it-alls with their endless advice." There was so much pressure on the children to do well: "The parents acted like they were the ones playing the sports. That drove me nuts; it took the fun out of it." Helen also noted an interesting schism between these "really athletic kids and their grossly overweight parents. I didn't get the connection." At times, the displaced parental pressure was so great that, "we weren't enjoying it at all—the kids weren't and I certainly wasn't. We all felt bad. It was just bad. It's just hell. Sports are hell!"

Fundraising also caused friction for Helen and her family, as Helen lives in an affluent area of town. "The fundraising was a joke. Parents would show up for bottle drives in their Cadillacs. Most parents just ended up coughing up cash rather than fundraise." Bad Mommy was really happy when those sports days ended.

Chapter 35

Hip Bad Mommy

One of the biggest obstacles faced by a mommy is coming to terms with her own physical identity post-baby. She may have "discovered" herself and her "look" as a single person, but her character as a mommy is an entirely new construct. Is she Madonna? Or is she a whore? Or is she a Madonna-whore? Depending on how old you are when you have your first child, it can be a challenge to reassert your fashion sense in your postpartum body. Besides all the new rolls and bumps, there is also the new role as a mommy to be considered.

Some mommies choose the path of least resistance. With her first pregnancy, this type of mommy will adopt the large sweatshirt and overalls that will become her uniform for the next twenty years. Quick access to the breast is paramount, and all other considerations fall by the wayside. Realizing that her years will be filled with vomit spills and urine stains, she also embraces a polyester wardrobe and abandons all fashion wisdom for the sensible world of wash and wear. This mode of dressing signals to the rest of the world that she has dropped out of society and has become a mommy (a good one, of course). By adopting this sense of fashion, she will be illustrating for her young that once a woman becomes a good mommy, her role has been completely defined. Her sense of individuality and spontaneity are gone by this point and she has been willingly co-opted into the Cult of the Mommy.

Some women will fight this inevitable trend with every fibre of their bodies. Instead of conceding fashion defeat gracefully, they will fight it every step of the way. These desperate creatures can be easily spotted in the hallways of the school by following the leers of the school daddies at drop-off time. These "yummy mummies" will often dress inappropriately for school, showing cleavage, thigh, and wearing little leather skirts and pointy stilettos to sports days (so hard to run over a wet field!). The pathetic yummy mummy is most often stuck in the era in which she turned sixteen and can thus be dated by considering the fashion accoutrements she wears. Yummy mummies have the goal of becoming cougar mommies in their children's teen years, as they pathetically attempt to become physically attractive to the peers of their own children. They will dress younger and younger as their children approach the age in which they themselves are permanently stuck. The yummy mummy is in extreme danger of becoming a cougar mommy as she hits the thirty-five-year benchmark, forever scarring her children with mortification over their mother's desperate and pathetic attempts to "look hot" despite her advancing years and the potentially preying behaviour towards their peers.

Mommies who have not come to grips with the fact that their bodies post-children will never be the bodies they had before birth, and sixty-odd pounds are a disturbing warning to the rest of us. Repeat this mantra with me: "Buying clothes that are too small makes me look fat." Having a striped and stretched belly muffin-top hanging over a two-sizes-too-small pair of low riders in the school hall just isn't good for anyone.

Mommies who don't try to be hip in any way, shape, or form are dooming their children to a similar fashion failure as adults. However, we have to remember that mommies who try too much are doing even more damage. One of the most important developmental tasks of the child is to rebel against the mommy. If the mommy is overly hip, the child will rebel by becoming a complete nerd. It is a narrow path we tread, fraught with dangerous waters on both sides.

Colleen, a forty-two-year-old mommy of a six- and nine-year-old, is a true "hip mommy." "Most Mommies need a style makeover," she begins. "I'm sad that some mommies age before their time. They may only be in their thirties, but they dress and act like they are in their fifties." Despite being besieged with pregnancy weight and lack of funds, Colleen has always had it going on. "I've always had good natural hair—it's my secret beauty weapon.... It's really hard to be hip when you are fat and nursing. And I don't mean overweight, I mean fucking ginormous!" Another trick for mommy survival is focusing funds on items that will last: "You can't afford to spend money on something you hope will fit you for only the next five minutes." Pregnancy and nursing clothes are "black and stretchy. Period."

Colleen has no qualms about being a hip mommy. "I do try to dress younger; I do it on purpose. I want to get away with it and I do...I now dress as though I am about ten years younger than I am." Colleen will not let being a mommy pull her down. "I check out the other mommies at school. All they wear is sweatpants—that's it. What's with these people? Do they not go to work?" There is truly nothing more sad and pathetic to Colleen than a Mommy who has given up. "Really, is one or two little pregnancies all it took for you to concede defeat?"

Krissy, a forty-year-old mother of teens, admits she's "desperate to be a hip mommy." Her biggest dream is "to be mistaken for my daughter's sister. In the olden days, I used to want to get carded at the liquor store; now all I can hope for is that someone thinks we are sisters." Fortunately, this marvellous event has occurred for this bad mommy on more than one occasion due to her daughter's mature looks and Krissy's "obsession with youth culture."

Despite an avowed love for the eighties—"the time when I rocked it"—Krissy studies today's culture for fashion cues. "I can't really pull off a Lady Gaga, but I try." Sometimes her daughter is embarrassed by what she wears: "If she asks, 'Mom, are you really going out like that?' I know I'm onto something good," confesses the bad mommy. Krissy recently got her first tattoo in a self-admitted "pathetic grab for my fleeting youth." She attempted to get her teen daughter to join her for a matching one, and her daughter flatly refused. "If I'm doing it, it obviously sucks," explains Bad Mommy.

Krissy feels that fashion is "unkind to those who have given birth." She feels that the whole low-slung jeans thing is an affront to stretch marks. Jeans, in general, are an ongoing issue of concern for Krissy, although she has new-found joy in jeggings, which she says "are like stretch jeans from heaven." Krissy says she can overlook a little camel toe if the pants will give her that svelte silhouette no Spanx will ever match. Krissy feels it is her life's mission to become a Yummy (Bad) Mummy. She is considering having "MILF" as her next tattoo.

Chapter 36

Bad Mommy Bullies

One of the biggest challenges for bad mommies is dealing with little bitches. Fresh in recovery from her own horrendous childhood and school experiences, Mommy is often shocked to see her own child being bullied at school. Of course, when we mommies were children, no one called it bullying, it was "learning to get along with others." Now, bullying has its own day, T-shirts, and websites.

The natural inclination for a mommy whose child is bullied is to take that other child behind the school and give him "what for." Alas, this is frowned upon in society and could lead to legal charges against Mommy—definitely not good. This is also true for online bullying. Mommies, no matter what, do not go and write something nasty on the bully's Facebook wall. IP tracking will be the death of you. Consider yourself warned.

Some mommies might find themselves on the phone to the bully's parent, trying to duke it out mommy-to-mommy. This technique will fail as well, as the mommy of the little bully is likely also a bully and may report this heinous infraction to the "mommy posse," leading to further ostracizing for both Bad Mommy and her child. It's important to note that bullying also exists within the mommy cohort. Certain mommies, with their carefully prescribed and stratified control of power, resources, and connections, rule the schoolyard and PAC (parental advisory council). These "power mommies" are often the parents of little bullies. Mommy may suffer a social blow from which she will never recover should she attempt to take on one of these divas and their evil little offspring.

In the olden days, children were left to "deal with it" on their own. Mommies who choose this dangerous path may have teenage suicide attempts and charges of parental psychological neglect on their hands. Letting kids deal with it is tantamount to abuse in our bullying-obsessed culture. The media is full of dire stories of parents who ignored the signs of bullying and depression, only to end up with a suicidal child on their hands, Bad Mommy.

On the other hand, getting involved is also the path to mommy ruin. Bullying can bring out the true psycho in some mommies. The media is full of stories of mommies who have decided to fight bullying head-on, going undercover in the world of teens to offer retribution to the local teenage bully. This is an extremely dangerous practice and likewise may lead to legal charges and suicide attempts by all parties involved. At the very least, in either case, the school and related staff and counsellors will black-list Bad Mommy for her over- or under-involvement with her teen's social development.

Some mommies are so overwrought by bullying that they choose to home-school their child to avoid this pitfall. Please, mommies, do not fall into this trap! Home-schooling will only delay the inevitable. "Bitches be bitches," and the sooner we learn to deal with it, the better.

As a thirty-eight-year-old mother of seven, Bad Mommy Suzanne has dealt with bullies for years, both within her own family and in the wider social network of children. Suzanne says, "Girls are the worst. Boys punch each other and they are done; they are best friends the next day. But girls are nasty. They put each other down, they make each other cry, and they bully by exclusion." Suzanne feels that girls are fundamentally "herd" creatures and work in large groups with a strong leader. These "power bitches" need to be identified and avoided at all costs.

Suzanne has attempted to deal with the bullies by calling their mommies directly. This is a dismal failure, as most mommies do not take kindly to having their children's faults pointed out to them. "The mommies are no better than their children. That's where they learned it from in the first place," explains Suzanne.

Suzanne, with a mixture of chagrin and pride, admits to taking matters into her own hands. As a member of the Parent Advisory Council who is in charge of "hot lunch" and "cupcake day" at school, she has, on more than one occasion, used this power position to threaten a bully. "I pulled the little offender close to me in the cupcake line and whispered, 'Leave my daughter alone or you will never eat hot lunch and cupcakes in this school again!'" The children all now know Suzanne and the power she holds in the school. Her children are generally treated well or completely avoided; both are acceptable scenarios to this bad mommy.

Thirty-nine-year-old Maeve is the mother of a ten-year-old daughter and fourteen-year-old son. Her son has been bullied over the years because of a mild developmental disability. "Bullies go after the perceived weak links, and special needs kids have a huge target on their backs." Maeve sees many kids as "walking targets...new kids, fat kids, kids with accents, and weird kids. If you have a weakness, they will find it." Bad Mommy feels that children who bully generally come from families where difference is not tolerated and accepted: "It's not really their fault."

Maeve will go "into mama bear mode" when her child is threatened. "It's a natural defence. We are programmed to do this." Recently, Maeve's child was called "retard" at school. Maeve was irate when this was reported to her: "I thought, 'Those little bastards.' I just wanted to kill them." However, being a good mommy, Maeve went to speak to the teacher directly. "The teacher was fantastic and held a classroom intervention." The identified bully admitted to using the "R word," and Maeve was invited into the class to talk about disabilities and issues of diversity. "Bullying will happen and kids should learn to handle it to some degree—we are all little jerks sometimes—but if it's about issues of diversity, we need to step in. Even adults need help and support with that stuff."

Chapter 37

Bad Mommy and New Media

Life is complicated for bad mommies. When we were teenagers, communication happened verbally or by notes furtively passed in the hall. There was no electronic trail of poor congress damning us for eternity on the internet. Nasty lines of texting were simply incomprehensible—the closest thing to this might have been a few lines in the bathroom stall that would be painted over by the school custodian by the end of the week.

All children over the age of six seem to have cellphones and Facebook. Children tweet their breakfast requests to befuddled parents who struggle with complicated computer activities, such as attaching photos to emails. This new media presence is leading to a new, complicated parenting wrinkle—and one that no amount of Botox can fix.

Many bad mommies have no real idea how to function with new media in the first place. Everyone knows that if you can't figure out your cellphone or computer, then you get your child to fix it. This can be problematic when Mommy is trying to figure out what her child is up to on the internet and has no idea how to even log into the computer that the same child has carefully password protected from Mommy.

To complicate things further, many mommies, in their desire to be hip and "dialled in," wish to communicate with their children using the parlance of new media. This leads to awkward issues such as her "poking" her child on Facebook and making erroneous assumptions after reading chat transcripts left up on the family computer. Should Mommy be her child's "friend" on Facebook? Should she "friend" the friends of her child? Just because you have known them since preschool doesn't mean they want you looking at pictures of them getting wasted or knowing what kind of "porn star" they are. There is nothing cool about stalking your child and their friends on Facebook, no matter how tempting it might be!

While pathetic attempts at being involved in new media as a parent will land Bad Mommy in hot water, looking the other way and pretending it doesn't exist will lead to a complete breakdown in parenting. If not for texting, many families would cease to communicate at all. Parents who ban computers and cellphones in the home are setting up their child for failure in the "real" world, where no one apparently ever communicates directly anymore.

As if it wasn't bad enough that Mommy now has

to learn all about computers, allowing them into her house also, apparently, is an open invitation to a world of sexual predators out to hunt down and kidnap her children, via wireless modem! Even if you are clever enough to install Net Nanny or some other form of pervert firewall, a real predator will simply scoff at your efforts. Did you know that webcams can be turned on remotely? That means that a perv can actually turn on a webcam in your house—in your child's bedroom!—and watch to their little vile heart's content. With any luck, they might actually take screenshots from your child changing and put them up in pervy chat rooms for all to "enjoy." Awesome…and you were thinking you were being so good setting up a webcam so that little Stephanie could chat with granny in Australia.

Please, do not overly fret about these horrific issues, mommies. If you provide a computer for your child, you will open them up to a world of online bullying, perverts, and internet addiction. If you do not, your child will be damned for eternity to a blue-collar job—at best—and, most important, less than one page of Google hits for their name! It's all really just a matter of personal choice.

Krissy, a forty-year-old bad mommy of two teens, admits to being "a complete idiot" when it comes to the internet and so-called "new media." Krissy has a tremendous fondness for her Tandy computer from the early eighties and hasn't really gotten with the times since then. Despite her self-proclaimed ignorance, Krissy's family members are "early adaptors" of new electronics. But this is entirely driven by her partner and teens; Bad Mommy is merely "along for the ride."

Although admittedly ignorant, Krissy does depend on her cellphone and computer for regular contact with the outside world. The only problem, she says, is "my children have set up the entire program for me." Bad Mommy has no way to keep communication private or sacred, as her young set up the whole password system, including actually choosing the passwords, because she "forgot the whole add numbers and symbols thing. Like it's not complicated enough already. I mean, come on, numbers AND symbols?"

Most of the time, all is well with the family computer unless there are no teens around to fix it. Krissy has recently tried to get "hip" with texting and has been texting her daughter at school, even using text shortcuts she read in an online forum. Her daughter asked her to "just forget it" and call her instead. Krissy also tried to "sext" her husband the other day with her new phone by taking a racy cleavage shot. Unfortunately, she sent it to all her favourites instead of just her husband. Not cool. To make matters worse, the picture got added to the family photos on iPhoto and is regularly mocked by her teen and her friends.

Krissy desperately wants to "get with the program" and recently had her teens create a blog for her, since, as she says, "all the cool mommies are blogging these days." She was extremely proud of her blog, which she felt was very high-tech and even included some uploaded photos and links. She was thus mortified when her teen informed her that "no one is blogging anymore" and mocked her for not having her own YouTube channel. Krissy now has her own YouTube channel, but doesn't have any content on it. She says it's because her children have given up on her and refuse to help..."little ingrates." She joined Twitter and tried to tweet but "couldn't figure out the point of the whole thing." Bad Mommy wants to go back to the "good old days" when people actually spoke to each other and wrote letters.

Forty-three-year-old Abigail is the mother of a six-year-old daughter. She and her family introduced their daughter to the internet and technology at an early age. They registered their daughter's full name as a domain at birth but had to settle for a "dot-net," as the "dot-com" was already taken. "It's an investment for the child's future when you think about it!" says Abigail.

Abigail feels that she and her family are "very tuned in and very interconnected." Her daughter has also had her own email since birth but doesn't know how to access it. At this time, her daughter needs help "logging in," since she doesn't know the passwords to the computer, but Abigail admits that her six-year-old cheerfully "downloads apps to her own iPad and iPhones" and only checks with Bad Mommy "if she has to pay for them and needs a password." Abigail's six-year-old has understood from an early age the power of e-commerce. "Let's just get it on eBay!" was an early and oft-uttered phrase by her young tot. Abigail feels that children should know how to use these powerful tools. Her daughter started using a mouse when she was two years old and would say "just click it" when any sort of problem arose—online or not. Abigail's daughter made a Valentine's Day card for her parents this year. It read, "I love you because Dadda plays video games with me and Mamma watches television with me."

Abigail would like it known, for the record, that she does limit "screen time." If her daughter has screen time during the day, "her behaviour is appallingly bad. Screens are like a drug; if you have a dose in the morning, you are jonesing for the rest of the day."

Chapter 38

Bad Mommy Tackles Teen Sex

Nothing raises the hackles of a mommy like the thought of her own teen engaging in sexual activity. Unfortunately, we were all teens at one time, and we clearly remember both the "jiggery" and the "pokery" in which we engaged behind our parents' backs. While that was all good clean fun back in the day, when it comes to our own children, abstinence and convents seem more and more attractive with each passing day.

Teenage sexuality is threatening for a number of reasons. First, the very idea of someone you have breastfed engaging in sex is a fundamentally repulsive notion. However, it's the potentially nasty side effects of sexual activity that most threatens Bad Mommy—disease and pregnancy and, of course, a bad reputation. Should your child get knocked up, that would make Mommy a—*shudder*—Grand-Mommy! Either that or a charming mother-daughter visit to the local "family planning" centre is just around the corner.

Some bad mommies deal with the angst and anxiety of teen sex by practicing full openness and disclosure regarding sexuality: *The Joy of Sex* is a frequently thumbed-through coffee-table book, and new boyfriends and girlfriends are invited for sleepovers, as long as they use protection. By practicing such lax parental control, these mommies hope to "keep their children safe" and espouse that "they are going to do it anyway, it might as well be some place safe and warm." These mommies will know where their children are but may also be exposed to such side effects as used condoms, overhearing sex noises, and the uncomfortable realization that they are getting old.

Other bad mommies use a diametrically opposed tact and encourage their child to participate in chastity-based programs. Dire warnings of opposite-sex frolicking and heavy chaperoning of any potentially sexual endeavours lead these children to be extremely subversive in their sexual behaviour. The more a mommy tries to contain her child's sexuality, the more this same child will find a way to express it.

Mommies, you are damned if you do and damned if you don't. The safest route for you is to leave home when your children are sixteen and check in again when they are twenty-five years old.

Suzanne, a thirty-eight-year-old bad mommy of seven (including several teens), says, "Teen sex is not a fun subject." She had her first child when she was eighteen years old and thus her platform for advocating teen sexual abstinence was out the door before she even started. Her twenty-year-old son started dating when he was seventeen—not bad—but the girlfriend was fifteen.

Suzanne told him, "You're going to go to jail." Her son and his girlfriend spent a lot of time downstairs in the "games" room, and Suzanne came up with a number of techniques to ensure that no naughtiness occurred. First, she removed all blankets, as blankets were a clear "route to naughty behaviour." Second, she would yell downstairs to clap periodically, so she would know that their hands weren't doing something else. The rhythmic sound of clapping from the basement led Bad Mommy to feel confident that nothing was going on...until one day when she was downstairs doing laundry where the lovebirds couldn't see her. She ordered them to clap and saw them each use one hand to make the clapping sound. Bad Mommy shudders to consider what the other hands were up to.

Suzanne also walked in on her son and girlfriend in a disrobed state once after forcing in the bedroom door. It had been blocked by a dresser. She thought: "I'm just going to die." They were "giggling like crazy. She didn't have a shirt on and he wasn't wearing pants." Suzanne is powerless to stop this. Her son always says, "You had me when you were eighteen. You can't tell me anything." Alas, he's right.

Helen, a forty-nine-year-old mother of two daughters, nineteen and twenty-one, had one firm rule: "Don't let them date in high school." She explains that teenagers just "aren't emotionally ready for the inevitable breakup and will be devastated." That being said, Helen expects a certain amount of teenage sexual activity. The key to this, she says, "is to always give them their privacy. Once you take that away, you are fucked." In truth, Bad Mommy doesn't want to know what her daughters are really up to any more than she wants them to know the details of her private shenanigans.

Alas, this tactic may have backfired somewhat. Her nineteen-year-old daughter has never dated and is "worried that it's never going to happen." Helen's not sure how her daughter expects to meet anyone, as she is always on the computer or on the couch: "If you want to meet a boy, it's not going to happen on the computer." Helen says she "kind of lied about sex" to her daughters: "Not wanting to tell them the truth about their periods, I just told them it was mostly water, not blood." Bad Mommy explains, "I like to lie to them; I think it's better." She is pretty sure that her daughters know about pregnancy and how it's caused but has no idea how they came to that information. Helen says she "tried to tell them, but they don't want to know. It completely grosses them out...they get the info in the streets. That's best."

Helen is relieved that high school is over. She was horrified by some of the girls in her daughters' high school: "Holy shit, girls have bigger tits now. You should see these girls. They all look like porn stars." Her daughters' school stopped holding high school dances because "girls were giving blow jobs in the bathrooms. Not cool for school."

Chapter 39

Bad Mommy and Teenage Wasteland

Mommies, do you remember being a teen? Didn't we have a great time getting wasted with our friends? The bong hits, the shots and lines, the projectile vomit in the back seat of the car...doesn't that make you misty-eyed? What would the teen years be without getting wasted? Of course, back in Mommy's day, getting wasted involved a six-pack and a dime bag of Columbian. These days, the stakes are much higher with roofies and crystal meth taking all of the fun out of a little after-school playtime.

Once again, the spectre of hypocrisy rears its ugly head for Mommy. While we loved nothing more than cutting classes to huff a fatty in the hot box, heaven forbid we encourage or even deign to acknowledge the same behaviour in our own children.

Some mommies feel that denial and lies are a poor excuse for parenting. They foolishly believe that a truthful, full disclosure of their own youthful naughtiness will build a trust and rapport with their own teens. These are the mommies who will prepare vodka Jell-O shots for their teen's football team's after-party in the hopes of being seen as a "cool mommy." This will, of course, fail miserably. Although there is something attractive about a forty-something woman with over-frosted hair doing Jell-O shots with teens, in the end, she will simply be fodder for laughter, wet dreams, and, potentially, charged with administering a noxious substance to a child. As well, mommies who disclose their own past relationships with drugs and alcohol now have no leverage at all against their own children, who will rightly charge them with hypocrisy.

Knowing this painful truth, many mommies practice the "lie and deny" technique of parenting, professing only mild experimentation with red wine at dinner after the age of twenty-one. These mommies will carefully comb through yearbooks and other potentially damaging archives of teenage naughtiness and cull any evidence of parental wrongdoing. These mommies are setting up their family for disaster. While it's true that their children, thinking (wrongly) that Mommy won't recognize that water bong for what it really is, will not try so hard to hide drug paraphernalia, their children will also feel that they can never come to their parent with any substance-related concern or question. These children will be the most likely to end up wasted at a party, having ingested God knows what. If only they had felt able to ask Mommy whether Purple Haze bud should have sticky resin on it or not, things might have ended up better for everyone.

Krissy, a forty-year-old mother of two teens, admits she is "terrified" her teens will find out about her long-standing relationship with drugs and alcohol. She recently read somewhere that addiction is inherited through the father, which has given her some modicum of relief, as her own teen years and early adulthood were full of "partying and blackouts."

Now that Krissy's own children are the age she was when she began her "horrific yet delicious downward descent into addiction," she watches them, hawklike, for symptoms of use. Krissy surreptitiously examines their eyes for telltale glossiness and subtly sniffs their collars when they come in for a kiss at night. Bad Mommy admits to rifling through their drawers and backpacks, but justifies this as being for their own good. After all, she knows first-hand just how naughty teens can be.

In order to keep her children away from experimenting with drugs and alcohol, Krissy has carefully planted some pieces of misinformation in their brains. She recently told them that "ninety-five percent of all marijuana sold on the streets is laced with crystal meth and that with one toke of this meth-laced pot you will be addicted forever." Bad Mommy is "straight edge" herself (these days) and brashly espouses the "clean lifestyle" while brushing away any questions about her own not-too-recent past. Krissy regularly drives her teens around the "dodgy" parts of town, pointing out homeless people and diagnosing their drug and alcohol history. She cruises her teens' friends on Facebook, looking for symptoms of "partying" and taking screenshots to share with these teens' parents.

Krissy recently learned that a medication exists to treat alcohol addiction: if injected with the medication, the patient will vomit profusely if they drink alcohol. She is actively looking into having this injected into her own teens on a prophylactic basis. Krissy suspects some of her teens' friends' parents are allowing teens to drink and party in their homes. She plans to track these parents down and charge them with "administering a noxious substance." Krissy believes with extreme anxiety that her own children are one sip or toke away from complete depravity. She should know—she's their Mommy.

Keira, a fifty-year-old mother of two young adults, admits to some decidedly alarming behaviour involving her children and the use of drugs. A self-proclaimed "hippie," Keira espouses a philosophy of "experimentation and saying 'yes,' within reason." Keira and her partner struggled with the behaviour of their then five-year-old daughter. She was hyperactive and demanding and all parenting interventions were unsuccessful: they attempted time outs, putting her in a corner, star charts, and behaviour modification. Keira's partner at the time was working in a group home with emotionally disturbed children and applied all of the techniques he picked up on the job to their daughter to no avail.

At last, her partner suggested, "Maybe if she smokes a little joint, that will kind of calm her down." They sat their child down and took turns blowing marijuana smoke in her face and instructed her to inhale deeply. Alas, her "hyper and ratty" behaviour did not stop; instead, she become totally hysterical and panicked and claimed she couldn't feel her legs. Bad Mommy and her partner thought, "Oh fuck, what are we going to do now?" and it occurred to them that hydrotherapy might be the answer. They drew a deep, warm bath and put their daughter in it, singing to her softly in the dark until she "came down" and the feeling returned to her legs.

Years later, Keira tended her own marijuana patch and had her daughters assist her in gardening, including sexing plants and hiding them from the helicopters overhead. Although her eldest daughter eschewed drugs in all ways, her youngest became a pot fiend in her early teen years. Keira wasn't too impressed and requested that she "keep it to the weekends and after homework was done." Bad Mommy's new boyfriend and the daughter had their own outdoor "grow show" going, and Keira thought: "I couldn't stop them. It was fine; I never felt bad about it." Keira didn't want to be a hypocrite. "It's like the French and wine," she explains. "You start them young and reasonably, and it never gets out of hand."

Chapter 40

Bad Mommy Moves Out

There comes a time in the life of a mommy when her child needs to spread her wings and leave the nest (thank God.) While this used to occur around the child's eighteenth birthday, to coincide with the end of high school, the new crop of "fledglings" are leaving the nest later and later. Bad Mommy is lucky if her beloved baby moves out by age twenty-five, and more and more commonly, baby doesn't move out until their early thirties. This delayed adolescence can be problematic for Mommy on many different levels. We grew up learning to be parented until we moved out at age eighteen and were thus treated as adults. If our children never move out, then they never learn to be adults. Mommy also never gets to have the mommy-time she has longed for all these many decades. The pot of gold at the end of the parenting rainbow never ever arrives, as the end point continuously move further away.

Some bad mommies have the enviable position of living with both their grown children and their own parents. These mommies have never grown up and reached independence, and their own children have also never left and reached independence. This cruel sandwich of parenting refuses to allow any member of the family to manifest their own destiny, all in the name of "familial support and love."

Many mommies still hang onto the hope of their child moving out. As the day their child graduates approaches, they collect university and college catalogues from distant shores, hoping to entice their child into moving far, far away. While some of these mommies are successful in this endeavour and do lose their child at age eighteen, they will pay for their insolence, as these far-flung teen-adults will likely never move back to their home city or even country again, stealing Bad Mommy's future grandchildren and position as family matriarch from her forever-more. These long-distance children will adhere to their new partners' families, who will replace Mommy in their hearts and lives forever. Moreover, late-night calls involving pregnancy and vomiting and/or the police cannot be dealt with easily when Mommy is half a country away. These mommies do have their freedom but have kissed their futures good-bye.

In contrast, clingy mommies just can't seem to ever let go. They encourage their children to attend school in their local town, stating it will save on "housing costs." Really, Mommy just doesn't want to cut the strings. These mommies can also be seen encouraging their children to obtain graduate degrees and even post-doctoral work, all with the secret conspiratorial plan to keep their children at home as long as possible. Some of these mommies are lucky enough to have children who are loners . and would never move out in the first place unless forced to. These mommies will often renovate existing homes to create child traps known as "basement suites" in order to keep their child in a fetal-like state hidden in the basement as long as possible.

Our forty-year-old bad mommy of teens, Krissy, is "petrified of my birdies leaving the nest." Although she is admittedly weary of parenting, she feels that "children moving out is the first nail in your coffin. First, they move in with friends and then you get sick and die." Parenting has been her whole life for the last twenty years: she wouldn't know what to do with herself if her children weren't in her home. Krissy didn't trust her children to make good decisions when they were young and doesn't see why she should change her opinion now just because they are a little older. Krissy also admires cultures that live intergenerationally. Although she personally would "rather die than live with my mother-in-law," she thinks it might be OK to have her own daughter- or son-in-law live with her...so long as the whole "worship the mother-in-law thing was in effect."

In order to fulfill her long-term fantasy of having her children live with her as adults, Krissy realizes she will need a larger home. The last thing she wants is to hear her children having sex. Unfortunately, housing costs being what they are, Krissy isn't sure if this is realistic. She notes that most large intergenerational houses live out in the sticks or in "some crazy cultlike compound somewhere in the Ozarks," and she isn't quite sure she is willing to go that far.

In the meantime, Bad Mommy keeps her children close by, citing high rents, crazy roommates, and unsafe streets. She lets her children know they can go to any university they choose as long as they can get to it by transit from her house. If Krissy plays her cards right, she can seamlessly segue from Bad Mommy to Bad Grand-Mommy with no child gap in between!

Keira, a fifty-year-old mother of two young adults, moved both of her daughters out as teenagers so that they could attend university in another town. Keira admits that she "didn't really think that one through. What the fuck was I thinking?" In retrospect, she feels it would have been better to move with her children. Her first daughter's transition to independence was relatively smooth. She moved in with a friend's family, and it seemed like a good situation. Unfortunately, though, on the five-hour trip to the new town, her daughter developed a migraine headache and Bad Mommy "just lost it with her. I mean, it was our last day together, and I was like, 'Fuck, Jesus, smarten up, I can't believe you are doing this!'" Denied her last supper with her daughter due to a pesky migraine, Keira found herself cross and vexatious.

Her second child's move to independence was even worse. This daughter had struggled the entire summer before moving out with extreme separation anxiety—she was only seventeen years old. Finally, in exasperation, Keira told her that "she could stay, but she would have to get a full-time job." That was evidently the kick in the pants that was needed, and her daughter agreed to move. The day of the actual move, Keira dropped her youngest off on a street corner with her older sister, now well established in the larger city. Her daughter became hysterical and "wouldn't let go of the car door. I literally had to peel her fingers off one by one as she screamed, 'Don't leave me!'" When Bad Mommy finally removed her child from the vehicle, she and her husband went to have a Chinese food dinner to eat crab together in order to recover. Yes, Keira felt bad, but the child had to go.

Eventually, with both girls gone, Keira felt great relief. She had been parenting non-stop for twenty-one years and was about to experience freedom for the first time. Then, less than a month later, her husband's ex-wife tried to "dump her son on them...a rangy, awful little boy." The ex-wife figured now that Keira's daughters were gone, she would have space for one more child. "I don't think so," replied Keira.

Conclusion

Mommies, remember this: in your struggle to be the best you can be, you will inevitably fail—just as all those around you fail each and every day, and just as every mother before you, in an unbroken bad mommy mitochondrial line back to Bad Mommy Eve, has failed. Be comforted in knowing this dark little truth and rejoice in the small glimpses of joy you may find in your mommy journey. Be secure in knowing that despite the platitudes and despite the greeting cards and the false Good Mommy Books, each and every one of us is truly and utterly bad. Your task in parenting is to be just a little less bad than the mommy before you. Nothing more....

In solidarity,
Willow